Geoffrey Squire

DRESS *and Society*
1560-1970

A Studio Book

The Viking Press · New York

To my mother

Originally published in England under the title
Dress Art and Society 1560–1970
Copyright © 1974 by Geoffrey Squire
All rights reserved

Published in 1974 by The Viking Press, Inc.
625 Madison Avenue, New York, N.Y. 10022

SBN 670–28484–x

Library of Congress catalog card number: 73–11542

Printed in Great Britain by
Fletcher & Son Ltd, Norwich

Contents

Acknowledgements

To record proportionate thanks to all the people, known and unknown, who have consciously or unwittingly contributed towards the ideas presented in this book would be impossible, but mention must be made of three inspiring teachers. To Miss Jeannetta Cochrane, Miss Norah Waugh and Miss Margaret Watts, all formerly of the old Central School of Arts and Crafts, I owe the firm foundation in the history and practicalities of costume upon which I have built in a way that I can only trust they would have approved.

More immediate thanks are due to my brother Kenneth for constant help and the quiet of his house, in which the major part of the text was rewritten during the splendid Norwegian summer of 1972; to Mr Charles Gibbs-Smith for much advice, and for reading the first draft; to Mrs Madeleine Mainstone, in charge of the Education Department of the Victoria and Albert Museum, for so generously allowing me to develop my theories in practical teaching, and to Mr Brian Finney of London University's Extra Mural Department, under whose auspices the lectures here adapted were first given, in the autumn of 1970.

I owe much to my many colleagues at the Victoria and Albert Museum, especially to Mrs Pat Connell, always ready to argue a point; to Mrs Celia O'Malley, who has carried out any number of dull chores, and Mr Bertie Maxwell of the Department of Prints and Drawings, whose patience is endless.

Thanks too to Miss Violet Sweet who undertook the labour of typing my text, and to Miss Sally Chappell who took many of the photographs.

I owe a deep debt to Mr Walter Lucas and Mrs Jean Holden of the British Drama League, and to Mr James Forsyth and Mr Anthony Cornish of the London Faculty of Tufts University who have always shown such faith in my ideas. To my many students I am grateful for such enthusiastic response in our work together, which has helped immensely towards the formation of this book.

My editors, Miss Frances Lincoln and Miss Frances Kennett have been

unfailing in kindness and patience during the sometimes traumatic transformation of lecture notes into publishable text.

Thanks are due to Mr T. W. I. Hodgkinson of the Victoria and Albert
Museum for more than he can know; and to Miss Angela Lewi of the
National Portrait Gallery, but for whose good offices this work would
probably never have been undertaken; also to the Committee of the
Costume Society for permission to use material originally published in
their Bulletins, to A. D. Peters and Company for kind permission to re-
print the passage by Rose Macaulay with which I close, and to the many
other publishers and galleries for permission to reproduce works. They are
acknowledged below.

Without all these kind people, and the friends who have pressed me to
publish *something*, this book could never have appeared. Anything of value
in it comes from the help, encouragement, criticism, enthusiasm and the
insights of others, and to all of them it is offered with deepest gratitude.

February 1973

Acknowledgements for illustrations

Ashmolean Museum, Oxford, pp. 22, 23, 92, 111; Bodleian Library,
Oxford, p. 28; Condé Nast, pp. 12, 14; Hardwick Hall, Derby, p. 50;
London Museum, pp. 52, 97; Mansell Collection, p. 43; National Gallery,
London, pp. 24, 30, 54, 68, 74, 90, 118; National Portrait Gallery, London,
pp. 16, 53, 60, 62; Northampton Museum and Art Gallery, p. 99; Statens
Museum for Kunst, Copenhagen, p. 137; Tate Gallery, London, pp. 81,
128; Trustees of the British Museum, London, pp. 12, 31, 61 (Crown
copyright); Trustees of the Wallace Collection, London, pp. 10, 42;
Victoria & Albert Museum, London, pp. 11, 17, 29, 30, 31, 32, 44, 51, 54,
56, 57, 63, 64, 67, 70, 76, 77, 79, 80, 82, 83, 85, 87, 88, 89, 91, 95, 98, 99,
100, 105, 107, 109, 112, 114, 115, 117, 119, 122, 131, 134, 139, 140, 141,
146, 150, 155, 158, 160, 162 (Crown copyright); Westminster Abbey,
London, p. 39; left-hand photograph on p. 12 was taken by Paul Rand
and photograph on p. 39 by Sally Chappell; illustrations on pp. 14, 48,
49, 72, 144, 149, 151, 156 belong to the author; illustrations on pp. 21, 36,
37, 38, 40, 47, 48, 80, 93, 96, 138 were drawn by the author.

Clothes; clothes; any old clothes?

Traditional Street Cry

. . . men at different times see with different eyes. Men see things differently in the morning than in the evening. The way in which one sees depends on one's mood.

Edvard Munch

The world is our picture. Only childish people imagine that the world is what we think it is. The image of the world is a projection of the world of the self, as the latter is an introjection of the world.

C. G. Jung

The eye of the beholder

The aim of this book is to present fashionable European dress of the past as an essential manifestation of changing patterns in thought and belief. Viewed in relationship to the other arts, clothing can be seen to be an integrated and characteristic expression of its period. Historians too often dismiss dress as of little importance and slight interest, unworthy of that careful consideration they give to architecture, sculpture, painting or literature. This is perhaps from an ingrained puritan prejudice against what may be regarded sensibly as 'at all times a frivolous distinction',[1] or the feeling that it can never provide a significant medium for expression and ought properly to be only functional and comfortable, or other reasons less definable. And yet, as Quentin Bell suggests,

> our whole conception of the world must be deeply influenced by
> the changing appearance of our fellow creatures.[2]

Conversely, one might say that our conception of the world must deeply influence our appearance. From either point of view we see that there is a powerful interaction between the world we live in and the appearance we choose to make within it.

This book attempts to redress what seems to be a common oversight by discussing fashionable dress as both an aesthetic experience, and as an essential expression of that generalized personality which emerges from a period. Like other arts, dress is the product of the creative imagination, transmuting the experiences of mankind into art which 'outlives the practical activities of an age, and endures as a permanent revelation of a people's aspirations'.[3]

Are clothes basically functional, and only unintentionally and fortuitously a medium for expression? If they are primarily a medium for expression what are the limits within which a composition may be regarded as clothing? Once we ask such questions we are confronted by one aspect of dress which has, indeed, attracted many philosophers each quite determined to force all nature to submit to his favourite theories.

1 Austen, Jane, *Northanger Abbey*, 1818, Chapter x.

2 Bell, Quentin, *On Human Finery* (London, 1947).

3 Dunwell, Wilfrid, *Music and the European Mind* (London, 1968).

Contemporary illustrations can
help to recreate the impression
of a costume's first appeal to the
beholder. (*Left: The Marquise de
Pompadour* by François Boucher,
1755. *Right:* silk dress of the
eighteenth century.)

Two examples to prove that the need for physical protection is not necessarily paramount in the way men dress: an Indian in body paint, from an engraving by John White, 1585 (*right*), and a fashion photograph from *Men in Vogue*, Spring/Summer 1970 (*below*).

One early attempt to formulate a philosophy of dress was Thomas Carlyle's *Sartor Resartus*. Among its flashes of insight is contained at least one definitive and famous statement:

> The first purpose of clothes was not warmth or decency – but ornament. . . . The first spiritual want of barbarous man is Decoration, as indeed we still see among the barbarous classes in civilised countries.

It seems indisputable that for both the primitive and the sophisticated an obvious delight in the decoration of the body has provided, since time immemorial, one of the principle characteristics distinguishing the human race from the rest of the animal world. All the evidence is against the view that Man is by instinct a Naked Ape. In spite of some current efforts to break what has become at least an ingrained habit it may well be as long again before Man ceases to be a Decorated Ape. Significantly, such current efforts are far from convinced or positive. We may take the example of one advertisement of September 1970, announcing that the very latest foundation garment would allow its wearer to 'look naked but feel fully dressed'.[4]

On this page are illustrated examples drawn from very different societies separated in time by approximately four hundred years. Clearly in neither does the need for warmth or any physical protection receive consideration. It *may* be that decency has been glanced at in the apron of the one, and *perhaps* receives lip-service in the other by the cutting of the photograph, but it is important to note that the exclusion of considerations of warmth or decency in either case does not *necessarily* make decoration their overriding purpose.

It must first be agreed that the drawing of a North American Indian, made in the late sixteenth century, shows neither fashionable dress (the subject of this study), nor purely primitive costume. It is specifically *customary* wear, being 'The manner of their attire and painting themselves when they go to their general huntings or at their solemn feasts'. Unquestionably its effect is decorative and controlled by aesthetic judgement. Nevertheless, ritual and symbolism have played a considerable part in the composition and are not intended to pass unnoticed. If the final result is considered only aesthetically its full message cannot be received.

Unlike the drawing of the Indian, the photograph from *Vogue* does not illustrate a current practice, but shows a dream imposed upon reality. An ambiguous sexual titillation and a delight in the mockery of a quite seriously appreciated extravagance are as much a part of its intention as any purely visual pleasure. Lord Chesterfield once wrote:

> . . . the difference between a man of sense and a fop is that the fop values himself upon his dress, and the man of sense laughs at it, at the same time that he knows that he must not neglect it.[5]

The creators of this image would seem to have been both men of sense and of sensibility to the spirit of our time and of its needs.

If the dress of the Indian may be said to be by intention highly serious,

4   *Barely There*, by Warner.

5   Chesterfield, Lord, *Letters to his Son*, 9 November 1745.

unaware of any foolishness, introvert and exclusive, and its decorative qualities to be incidental, in contrast the photograph is surely by intention frivolous, extrovert and inclusive. Its decorative quality, though not inconsiderable, *is* still incidental.

Only a few years before John White recorded the dress of the North American Indians, Michel de Montaigne was exercised in his mind in a 'chil-cold season, whether the fashion of those late discovered Nations to go naked be a custome forced by the hot temperature of the ayr . . . or whether it can be an originall manner of mankind'. After some debate he came to the conclusion that:

> . . . as those who by an artificiall light extinguish the brightnesse of the day, we have quenched our proper means by such as we have borrowed. And we may easily discerne that only custome makes that seem impossible unto us which is not so.[6]

This conclusion seems warranted by continual evidence that it is contemporary custom rather than contemporary climate which prompts the wearing of more, or of less clothing. The mind, knowing its body to be presenting the correct and acceptable visual appearance, will miraculously allow that body to endure, uncomplaining, seemingly impossible extremes of heat or cold.

The demands of decency or modesty are found to be of equal variability after the briefest study of almost any section in the development of European fashionable dress. The cod-piece may stand as an example. Introduced, as some evidence suggests, in an effort to preserve decency, it so riveted attention upon the area it was designed to conceal that gradually an exaggerated mimicry of the member resulted. This was apparently entirely acceptable to even the most fastidious and conservative of contemporary minds, but left behind pictorial records which proved a lasting puzzle and embarrassment to later generations.

Present experiments in transparent garments seem equally equivocal. It could be argued that the dress illustrated opposite would be less inflammatory, and considerably more honest than the high fashion of 1900, when frequently not even the face was left without an obscuring veil. But it would then defeat its own obvious aim, unless of course its *seemingly* obvious aim conceals a quite contradictory motivation and need – to reduce the potency of the female body by exposure. Mae West used to sing 'It's not what I wear, it's the way that I wear it; that's all brother, that's all!' The most nun-like wraps can prove indecent if the wearer intends to make them so. Complete nakedness, as in the symbolic picture of Truth, or the model for a 'life-class', may be utterly innocent. Usually it is manner not matter which matters. Modesty, like comfort or convenience is in the mind; in the mind of the observed as well as in that of the observer. Decency, as well as practicality, is a very variable attribute of dress.

An idea which has received the greatest support is that dress, far from being prompted by motives of decency, modesty or protection, was prompted on the contrary by a desire for display. Since costume became a subject for scholarly study, as well as a matter for personal taste and public

The cod-piece (*above*) was first introduced as a measure to preserve decency, but gradually developed into the most exaggerated mimicry of the member. (Engraving by Jost Amman from *Kunstbüchlin*, 1578.)

Present-day experiments with 'covering' seem as equivocal as the cod-piece: modesty, like comfort or convenience, is in the mind. (From *Vogue*, 1970.)

opinion, the most popular school of thought has attributed every possible variation to an effort to attract the 'opposite sex' – assuming generally that the opposite sex was male. 'Woman is the mould into which the spirit of the age pours itself'[7] James Laver has repeatedly assured us, and he, with a great majority, has concluded that the impulse to change is based on seduction. But history provides contrary evidence. Few, if indeed any of the elaborate disguises adopted by women secured immediate masculine approval, for men are in general extremely conservative in their preferences for what women wear, as most women know only too well. Naturally, when the initial struggle was over the disguises acquired attraction – from their association. But it was surely not the disguises which sexually allured – it was the idea of the women beneath them. Given the quite notoriously easy excitability of the male, if the main impulse in women's fashions is indeed seduction, she must have wasted a great deal of time, trouble and ingenuity carrying coals to Newcastle. One might have expected the emphasis on seduction to have been all the other way with *men* assuming extraordinary shapes in the hope of provoking the supposedly slower female response.

The theory of the Seduction Principle has not gone unchallenged, although naturally in a commercial society which has found sexuality so profitable, that challenge has received rather less than general notice. Doris Langley-Moore rightly pointed out, as long ago as 1949, that

all the psychological enquiries into fashion are predominantly concerned with feminine fashion and the band of theorists has without exception, been male.[8]

Meanwhile, the whole of literature was scattered with perfectly acceptable psychological comments to support another view, deduced by the light of nature long before psychology was formulated – and made often by women themselves. Mme de Lafayette, for example, observed in her novel *La Princesse de Clèves*:

When there is a party towards [the men] must reconcile themselves to taking second place for several days, because the woman does not exist who can give her lover a thought during the business of getting a new dress . . . it is all absorbing; and then this dressing-up is done quite as much to impress the world in general as for the sake of the loved one. Furthermore at the ball itself, it is their idea to be admired by all beholders, and the satisfaction they feel when they are aware of looking beautiful has little or nothing to do with their lover.[9]

All clothes inevitably have implications of sexuality, since clothes are intimately dependent upon the human body and can only be truly appreciated in that conjunction. The human body by its very nature must proclaim sex of some kind. That many clothes are sexually provocative *by intention* nobody could deny – but that others have had sexuality thrust upon them appears to be equally evident. The sexual allure emanating from the female court dress of 1600, or the masculine undress clothes of

6 Montaigne, Michel de, *Essays*, 1580, XXXV, 'Of the Use of Apparell'.

7 Laver, James, *Taste and Fashion* (London, 1937).

see also
Cunnington, C. Willett, *Why Women Wear Clothes* (London, 1941).

'In times past Woman has assumed some extraordinary shapes, sometimes that of the Great Pyramid, or that of a camel or even a wasp; in fact almost any shape was permissible except of course that of a woman. But the curiosities of shape were not accidental and each in its day secured the approval of masculine observers. . . . And, therefore, as presumably the basic elements of sexual attraction have always existed one must conclude that these elaborate disguises of the human form were in some way or another alluring.'

8 Langley Moore, Doris, *The Woman in Fashion* (London, 1949).

9 Mme de Lafayette, *La Princesse de Clèves*, 1672, translated by Nancy Mitford (London, 1962; reprinted by permission of A. D. Peters and company).

see also
Beerbohm, Max, *Around Theatres* (London, 1953); 'The Vesture of Mimes', 12 January 1901.

'. . . it is an utter fallacy to suppose that men's admiration of a woman is spurred by gorgeous frocks and jewels. On the contrary these accessories are obstacles to admiration. . . . Women dress elaborately to please themselves, or to please or displease other women. If they imagine that they please men by their elaboration they make a very great mistake. But probably they imagine no such thing.'

Sexual allure is certainly not the main aim of these two dress styles: female court attire, *c.* 1600 (*above*), and masculine undress, 1860 (*opp.*). (*Elizabeth I* by Marcus Gheeraets the Younger, *c.* 1592; the *Gazette of Fashion*, July 1860.)

10 Elyot, Sir Thomas, *The Book named the Governor*, 1531, Book Two, Section 3.

see also
Chesterfield, Lord, *Letters to his Son*, 9 November 1745.

'yet it is a very foolish thing for a man not to be well dressed according to his rank and way of life, for there are a thousand foolish customs of this kind which, not being criminal must be complied with, and even cheerfully by men of sense.'

1860, hardly strikes a modern eye with any force. The Freudians would probably reply that that is to beg the question; that the allure is necessarily symbolically proclaimed, and that humans know not what they do. But on the other hand humans do on the whole *think* that they know perfectly well, and surely the reasons for which we think we do things must count for something if not for everything? There is in any case a much more modish psychological theory, which suggests with all the force of novelty and exclusiveness that sexuality of the present human degree is an acquired and cultivated taste, and not an inherent natural characteristic. If this is so then modern dress has played its part in that cultivation. My purpose here is not to question the sexual significance of dress, but to enquire whether it must be considered at *all times* an equally overriding motivation, or whether on occasion it may be presumed to take second, third or even fourth place, giving precedence to some equally ever-present but momentarily more insistent demand. The garments illustrated here *may* be secretly loaded with obscure sexual significance, but is not the overt preoccupation with a 'seemly splendour' on the one hand, and a clear desire for physical ease and utility upon the other, of as great, if not greater significance?

The visual evidence of nineteenth-century masculine dress, when at last it began to be discussed, did in fact force the Seduction School into a tight corner, out of which it fought its way with the suggestion that male costume worked on quite different principles, and was motivated not by the need for physical display but by a desire to show respectability and the ability to support a family. These are conclusions which may be justified by nineteenth-century example but are hardly supported by any fashionable masculine wear before 1740, or after 1960.

However, this reasoning did bring the champions of sexual motivation part of the way to meet another school of thought whose founding father, by proxy, was I believe Quentin Bell. His ideas, with clear acknowledgement, were based upon the work of the economist Thorsten Veblen in *The Theory of the Leisure Class* which had appeared in 1899. Professor Bell's book *On Human Finery* added a fourth category to Veblen's list of the sumptuous motivations for clothing, bringing Conspicuous Outrage into company with Conspicuous Consumption, Conspicuous Leisure and Conspicuous Waste. The idea that clothes are in fact status symbols, intended to provide visible evidence of success, honour or circumstance, was something which almost anybody living before Freud would have been only too ready to admit. Sir Thomas Elyot had indeed admitted as much when, in 1531, in his *The Book named The Governor* he had written:

Apparel may be well a part of majesty. . . . So is there apparel comely to every estate and degree, and that which exceedeth or lacketh, procureth reproach, in a nobleman specially . . . it is expedient that a nobleman, in his apparel do avaunt himself to be both rich and honourable.[10]

Such views were widespread in the past, and must surely have accounted for quite as much as any unconscious and unacknowledged needs in the final appearance of men and women.

These are only some of the more feasible reasons suggested to account for the strange human custom of wearing clothes. To dwell further on these controversial matters would be to defer the main purpose of the book. Suffice it to say that so far no single motive can be awarded the undisputed honour of having originated dress or of providing its primary theme. Probably this is just. The human mind is complex and devious, and has always been subjected to many contradictory pressures. The civilization of Europe has been chiefly influenced by two very different early societies: the Ancient Greek and the Jewish.[11] The one was principally rational, the other almost totally instinctive, and their very different contributions have warred together for hundreds of years.

For the Medieval and Renaissance worlds, Man was the unique link in the Great Chain of Being, which stretched from the feet of God, down to the Earth, the cesspool of the Universe. In this Chain, Man was the only creature in whom the animal and the spiritual met and combined.[12] This old idea has not lost all justification or meaning. Is Man a Naked Ape? Or does the phrase, 'And they saw that they were naked', mean that men, seeing too clearly the possible consequences of their physical nature, chose to cover themselves, not to hide their shame, but to proclaim by that covering something of their aspiration to achieve also a full spiritual potential?

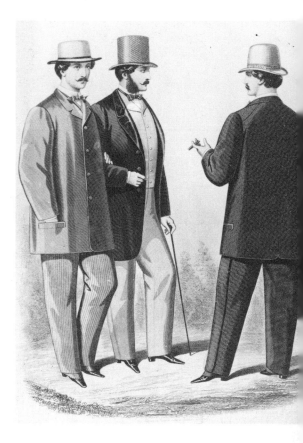

Almost entirely speculative, this book formulates ideas resulting from many years of enthusiastic response to clothes, in the hope that these may prove stimulating, provocative or useful to others who share both the enthusiasm and also my own misgiving that such an apparently frivolous preoccupation requires some intellectual justification. In my chosen field evidence may be gathered from three distinct sources, and a few remarks on each will show why an appreciation of the kind of objectivity they offer is the best argument for their complementary use.

First, there are authentic garments surviving from the past. Invaluable as the evidence is it would be a grave mistake not to remember its largely fortuitous character. Garments have been kept, more often than not, from motives of sentiment or association, both quite unconnected with any quality intrinsic to the clothes themselves. Some were put away, little worn, to be forgotten, having proved unsuccessful and never liked. Others were too complicated to be worth re-making, or were saved for some similarly arbitrary or accidental reason, and not because they were the most typical, or the best designed, or the most expertly cut and executed, of their age.

But, if we can accept that what survives represents general practice, in what sense does it represent appearance correctly? It seems to me that we must never lose sight of the fact that the human eye is always subject to the human brain, and it is for this reason that a second source of information must be invoked. Representational evidence ranges from painting and sculpture of the highest aesthetic quality to cheap and incompetent works, which are nevertheless instructive. It has been credibly proposed that until the Impressionists painted there were no blue shadows – only brown. Now shadows are usually blue.[13] Fanciful or not, there seems evidence enough that every age remakes the visible world to suit itself,

11 Halliday, Leonard, *The Fashion Makers* (London, 1966).

12 Tillyard, E. M. W., *The Elizabethan World Picture* (London, 1943).

13 Wilde, Oscar, 'The Decay of Lying', in *Intentions* discusses the effects of Impressionism on the mind (London, 1891).

and so has its own particular way of looking at the clothes which form its daily wear. The eyes of the beholders are so affected by their brains that they see not precisely what is before them, but what they wish to be there. This defect of vision seems to be produced in part by what has come to be known as the *Zeitgeist*, the spirit of the time, the mysterious force which results from communally held needs, beliefs and desires. But in part, too, it is produced by the persuasive second-hand vision of the world which acceptable contemporary artists and writers provide. 'The popularity of a piece . . . will always tell you more about the state of critical letters and public taste than it will about the excellence of the work.'[14] No dress that still exists can ever again look as miraculously smart or elegant as it did to the eyes of its period, when it was new; for in that magic moment, the period saw not only its fresh appearance, but added also what it wanted to see, making mental modifications to reality with encouragement from its creative artists, so that a perfection was seen which existed really only in the mind. Why else is it necessary to 'get our eye in' for a new style? Often what at first sight appears ugly and wrong will, after a short time and with increasing familiarity, grow less distressing until eventually it can appear the most beautiful, comfortable, hygienic and thoroughly satisfactory style that was ever invented.

The very nearest we can hope to get to this 'eye of the age' is by looking through the eyes of those contemporary artists who built the idealized vision into less ephemeral work. Certainly not all artists have been as sensitive to, or interested in, elegance and chic as were, for example, Carpaccio, Van Dyke or Boucher. Yet, though few can have had practical experience of tailoring or dressmaking, their observant eyes have often noted the precise details of seaming and construction as well as a characteristic pose calculated to display a costume to best advantage. The general impression at which the period aimed was probably exactly caught and held, and it is only by long and continuous looking at contemporary illustration that our imagination can be stimulated, and our eye encouraged, to see some hint of their first appeal in those garments which have miraculously survived. While, in general, it is secondary or minor artists who are concerned with the exact recording of contemporary dress, the *style* of the major painters who exploited personal invention or artistic license in matters of costume cannot be excluded from this category of sources. Such men as Michelangelo or Rembrandt gave far more than they received, yet could not have existed uninfluenced by the ages in which they lived.

Finally, there are written sources of information; inventories, accounts, letters, novels and plays, from which long and continuous reading can help to establish within ourselves something of the true feeling and outlook of a period – and inevitably its attitude to dress. But where evidence in writing is concerned we must note a tendency to comment or moralize which is necessarily more marked than in painting or sculpture, and which must be as warily approached as caricature. Attitudes of enthusiasm or disapproval involve extreme exaggeration which must be treated with reserve. Philip Stubbes[15] may be cited as typical of those who, making no attempt really to understand the spontaneous expression of their own day, can only shout abuse.

14   Albee, Edward, 'Creativity and Commitment', in *The Saturday Review* (New York, 4 June 1966).

15   Stubbes, Philip, *Anatomie of Abuses*, 1585.

'Their dublettes are noe lesse monstrous than the reste; for now the fashion is to have them hang down in the middest of their theighes or at least to their private members, being so hardquilted and stuffed, bombasted and sewed as they can neither worke, nor yet well playe in them, through the excessive heate thereof; and therefore are forced to wear them lose about them for the most parte, otherwise they could hardly eyther stoupe down or decline to the ground, so stiffe and sturdy they stand about them.'

Descriptions in words, even when favourable, rarely convey a clear visual impression. Clothes are essentially visual and need to be seen to be fully appreciated. What, for instance, can we gather from the following sentence?

Jean Muir moved with great control and dignity into a fuller, softer look, the ultimate refinement of peasant blouses in chalk white chamois leather, gathered and waisted, and classic caftans on which the sleeves spring out sideways from a vertical panel on the bodice.[16]

The description, typical of fashion reporting in every age, hardly makes a plain picture leap into the mind.

These then are the limitations even of evidence of primary quality. We can only learn to let the cumulative effect of all this evidence speak to us if we constantly weigh every aspect of its limitations. But still, without imaginative insight and interpretation, all fashionable dress deteriorates sadly into dead documents, to finish simply as old clothes.

16 Glynn, Prudence, *The Times* (London, 1 June 1971).

Our nature consists in movement; absolute rest is death.

Blaise Pascal
Pensées 1662

True style comes not from the individual but from the products of crowds of fellow-workers who sift and try and try again till they have found the thing that suits their native taste. . . . Style is ultimately national.

Hubert Parry
Inaugural address to the Folk Song Society of England, 1898

The human, visible, audible and intelligible media which artists (of all kinds) use, are symbols not of other visible and audible things but of what lies beyond sense and knowledge.

Ralph Vaughan Williams
The Letter and the Spirit

Style is the dress of thought

It is a paradox that changes of any kind, while prompted by a reaction *to* the familiar must yet be developed *from* the familiar. However apparently contrary the result, close links exist with what has gone before. Rarely indeed – perhaps not once in a thousand years – have new ideas, themes, techniques, appeared to spring from the mind of Man, seemingly complete and perfect, as Minerva was said to spring from the head of Jove. Mankind has built, carved, painted, sung, spoken and also dressed-up, often for centuries on end, using the same materials, the same principles, the same methods, the same types and the same subjects. Yet, miraculously, during those centuries Man's creations within each field have been continuously and subtly varied, one from another. His manner of expression has varied, even though his matter and his means have not. His style has changed constantly.

It may be debated whether an innovation in method or material occurs spontaneously, and more or less by accident, or whether it occurs at the prompting of some urgently experienced need or desire. It appears probable that the search for a different medium or technique begins only when the realization of some developing and insistent idea cannot be achieved fully by the currently available means. If Necessity *is* the Mother of Invention, then Desire is the Father. The demands of practicality are almost always simple. Clothes are to protect the body; a building affords shelter; words convey information. The requirements of mental and emotional satisfaction are far more complex. If Europeans dressed for over a thousand years in very slight variations on a loose-fitting, one-piece garment, this cannot have been simply because they lacked the ingenuity to make a garment fit. It would seem far more probable that no deficiency was felt; that no wish was present requiring a radically new experience; that there was no real need to give a bodily expression through the fitting of clothes closely, and so consequently no attempt to change was made. Unless a discovery answers some present problem or satisfies some current yearning, it will not be taken up, remaining the neglected brain-child of an eccentric. Only when an innovation, a theme, a statement, fits

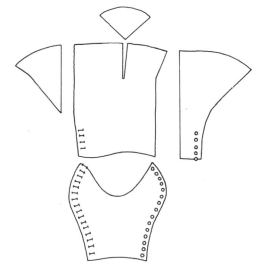

The five pieces which form each sleeve on the *pourpoint*, or doublet, belonging to Charles de Blois, *c.* 1360. (From the Musée Historique des Tissus, Lyons)

21

The manner of wearing the short gown and cloak is reminiscent of classical drapery, but this reinterpretation of an antique mode is achieved with garments of late fifteenth century form, when an elegant simplicity allowed the natural proportions of man to appear undisguised. (Attributed to Vittore Carpaccio, late fifteenth century.)

1 Panofsky, Erwin, *Renaissance and Renascences in Western Art* (London, 1965).

perfectly with the requirements of the mood of the moment, will it be noticed or exploited to its full capacity. It is surely significant that when Europe did at last apparently feel the wish to express itself through clothes fitted to define the body, a mere twenty-five years saw developments of such complexity that a single sleeve could be contrived from five, separate, subtly shaped pieces. Once the desire was felt, the means were found and speedily perfected. No obvious question of utility seems to have been involved in this decisive step, since in purely practical terms clothes which are not closely fitted are in general more convenient, more comfortable and less wasteful of material than clothes which are.

From such a viewpoint it appears that dress, quite as much as buildings, books or pictures, can be a manifestation of Man's urgent desire to express ideas and satisfy his mental needs, which transcend any consideration of physical comfort or convenience, and all considerations of sensible economy. In this way Man can alter the appearance of all things, including himself, to fit closely to an ideal, which, like the Ghost of Christmas Past, is always of dissolving parts, fluctuating in its distinctness.

One particularly clear and steady appearance of an ideal is embodied in the concept of the Renaissance – a complex series of adjustments in outlook and interests made by philosophers and artists during the fourteenth and fifteenth centuries. Adjustments, begun in the Gothic World, gradually created a totally new appearance for all men and their surroundings. The world was utterly changed. From traditional forms, materials and skills, newer forms were evolved, suitably to express themes seen from different angles or to emphasize neglected or unnoticed aspects. Earlier ideas, long forgotten or ignored, were not so much revived as reinterpreted. The appearance of the old was completely transformed and blended into the appearance of the new by the distinctive effect of style.

Although scholars and historians will argue about the details and the causes, the results and the influences or the exact beginning and the duration of such a changed appearance of the world, all are agreed that such a change occurred, and that contemporary minds and eyes were aware of it and affected by it.

> A period . . . may be said to possess a physiognomy no less definite, though no less difficult to describe in a satisfactory manner, than a human individual.[1]

It is therefore necessary to attempt to identify some of those period physiognomies which almost everyone recognizes, agrees about and names.

The most detailed section of this study will be concerned with that group of appearances in which the family likeness is so strongly marked that for a time all were together denoted simply by the single generic name – Baroque. Although agreement on absolute distinctions and precise naming remains tentative, continuing analysis has allowed several individualized faces to emerge from that collective mass which, for the purposes of this sketch, are to be identified as Mannerism; Roman Baroque; French Classical Baroque and Rococo.

It is not to be assumed that these form a series of separate, self-contained styles, one succeeding another in an ordered sequence, like the reigns of a monarchy, since all together constitute a continuation or development of their common progenitor, the Renaissance, and appear more, or less, distinctly in different areas at different times.

Superficially, the aristocratic and aloof intellectual artificiality of Mannerism gave place to the demanding, popular emotional power and illusionistic reality of High Baroque. In France, this was then disciplined into the formality of ceremonial and classical grandeur, which, in its turn, was later to soften into the intimate sensuality, the delicate playfulness of the Rococo. Such a brief résumé usefully draws attention to the usual cycle in which the *avant-garde* becomes the establishment. Boredom with the familiar requires the stimulus of the different. Again, this outline usefully brings out the changing emphasis on the intellect, the emotions and the senses in different epochs, but such a résumé is misleading where it suggests that all the characteristics associated with one style must be absent from the others, and that all the arts in all areas display exactly similar qualities at precisely the same time.

It was the Renaissance which provided the impetus and vocabulary upon which all these later styles depend, and the Renaissance was concerned above all with humanity in its fullest, widest, yet simplest sense. In the late Middle Ages, there had been 'an irreconcilable conflict between the life of the unsensual spirit and the unspiritual body'.[2] The concern of the new age was centred upon the rational; upon the scientific investigation of nature and the visible world; and upon the development of the human mind and body to their unified potential. While the body was to be brought to physical perfection and grace by exercise and control, this was not to be an end in itself, but formed the outward manifestation and counterpart to an inner perfection of the fully developed being. Balance and harmony between such a creature and his surroundings was to be achieved by the use of a natural human proportion in all things irrespective of scale. Professor Erwin Panofsky has pointed out that, because the parts of a column in a classical temple (the base, the shaft and the capital) are proportioned according to the relationship between the foot, the body and the head of a human being, a man is encouraged to 'expand his own ideal stature in accordance with the actual size of the building . . . whereas a Gothic cathedral . . . forces us to remain conscious of our actual stature'.[3] It was this concern with the human that caused men of the 1400s to turn back for inspiration to the Mediterranean Classical World, 'not so much out of any reverence for the Greeks and the Romans *per se* as because they found in the classics the most satisfactory expression of what they themselves were trying to express'.[4] This last point is important in relation to fashionable dress, for no obvious reference to, or imitation of the *forms* of classical clothing is to be found at any time during the age. In Italian fashions of the fourteenth and fifteenth centuries, however, there is evident an elegant simplicity which allowed the natural proportions and stature of the human to appear undisguised, and in masculine costume in particular the actual form of the body was displayed by closely fitted garments as at no other time since the Ancient World, when men had been often naked.

The new artistic culture of the fourteenth century appeared first in

2 Hauser, Arnold, *The Social History of Art* (London, 1951).

3 Panofsky, op. cit.

4 Read, Conyers, *The Tudors* (London, 1936).

Italy because that country was then the most powerful in Europe. There the organization of the financial and transport facilities of the Crusades had begun the revival of economic life. The first European banking system, the emancipation of the urban middle class, the development of free competition as opposed to the guild ideal of the Middle Ages, took place in Italy earlier than in the rest of Europe because feudalism and chivalry had been less well developed there than in the north. Rural aristocracy acquired town residences very early and adapted absolutely to the new urban financial aristocracy.[5] Conditions in Italy were exactly right for a seemingly fundamental break with the more immediate past. Also, in Italy the traditions of the classical world had lingered long on their native soil, and the Italians themselves lived their daily lives among the ruins of Rome. An appropriate inspiration was to hand. There was a confidence in the human condition which resulted in an expression of clarity, serenity, elegance and grace, and an assurance which required no forceful over-emphasis.

But it was not in Italy alone that the new spirit was stirring. All Europe felt the need for change from established institutions and ideals which had lost much of their original power and relevance. As Italy turned to her own earlier classical traditions, so the rest of Europe turned to Italy for inspiration and guidance.

The first freshness of vision of the early Quattrocento began to fill out with the Cinquecento into something more heroic and consciously noble. Buildings, and beings themselves, as they are portrayed in painting and sculpture, seem more powerful and dignified, more grave and solemn – still elegant and graceful – but yet heavier, more solid. So they must have appeared in life from the effect of their dress. The nobility and the dignity began to be consciously emphasized rather than left implicit, and the 'Grand Manner' of the High Renaissance appeared. From the consciousness of 'Grand Manner', it is a logical progression to the inflated grandeur of a showy theatricality, but such a development need not essentially be insincere, resulting as it may from extreme enthusiasm.

A theatre is a potent engine for working up the passions and the imagination of mankind; and like all such engines it is capable of the noblest recreations or the basest debauchery according to the spirit of its direction. So is the church. A church can do great things by precisely the same arts as those used in the theatre.[6]

By a stroke of fortune, at this point a visual comparison is possible which summarizes immediately the differences and dependencies of the arts of the Renaissance and the Baroque. In the 1480s, Mantegna painted *The Triumph of Caesar*: a work of individual genius and of élite scholarship, it typifies certain aspects of the Renaissance attitude and style. It has the cool, calculated, considered appearance of intellectual and scientific investigation. It is exciting in its suggestion of dignified and gracious splendour, but it is controlled. It sets out to reconstruct the appearance of the Ancient World by careful documentation and research, and because it does so, it carries more of the spirit of its own day than of the age it seeks to evoke. Being a scholarly reconstruction, filtered through a totally

In the sixteenth century, the image of the Renaissance began to fill out into something more heroic and consciously noble. (*Conte Sciarra Martinengo Cesaresco* by Moretto, *c.* 1540.)

5 Hauser, op. cit.

6 Shaw, George Bernard, Letter to W. T. Stead, 1904.

different mental outlook, it is refined, lacking that natural spontaneity which even a much inferior ancient Roman work would have. On the other hand, it has an immediacy all its own imparted by a powerful, noble imagination. It is not the journalistic record of a recent event, but a symbolic vision of a human possibility. It is informed by intellectual calmness, even though the artist views the excitement of a great victory parade. Its rich but muted colouring does not force itself upon the attention. Its drawing is precise, its technique firm. There is no hint of real ugliness or squalor in any of the creatures portrayed: the figures seem reminiscent of antique statuary, with smooth, taut limbs. Degree is observed but not emphasized. All is noble, majestic, considerate, and all is yet proportionate to human comprehension. There is no sense of strain or effort. We are not overwhelmed, although we are impressed. We are there, but may remain aloof while before us passes the procession, palpable, believable, but idealized and gravely quiet.

Compare the section containing the elephants with an adaptation made from it by Rubens, just over one hundred years later. There is so much the same, yet it is so very different. Here, all seems heat, excitement and noise. Only a sixth of the size of Mantegna's picture, it is more immediately demanding. We do not watch this parade go by, but feel swept into it. The rich colours strike the eye, provoking the senses. The handling of the paint is free, fluid and voluptuous. We can feel the silks and the smooth hide of the bulls, the tough leatheriness of the elephants' skins. We can hear the snarl and snorting of the animals and know that slobber drips and oozes from their mouths. The trunks flail, the torches flare and smoke, filling the air with the stench of their burning. Human flesh is full-blown and pneumatic. Calm nobility is overwhelmed by pomp and display and an opulent assertiveness. We are not asked to consider the splendour of a stately triumph – but are compelled to share in the abandon of victory. Mantegna had celebrated man at his full potential, as he is capable of being when senses and emotions are balanced by intellectual control. Rubens shows us man when intellect is thrust aside by passion and excitement. It is notable that while Mantegna chose to confine his composition to a perfect square, Rubens expanded his into a horizontal oblong which reinforces the sense of directional movement. Each picture has a different aim. Each records and provides a valid human experience. Other things being approximately equal, the differences of outlook, interest and ideal are conveyed by the differences in style.

While the grandeur of the Baroque was developed logically from the 'Grand Manner' and *gravitas* of the High Renaissance by a shifting emphasis, there were, within the 'Grand Manner', other possibilities ripe for development, or provocative of reaction. Kenneth Clark has suggested that a failure of nerve was evident among the younger generation of artists, when confronted by the sublime achievements of the early Cinquecento: either these must be slavishly imitated or totally rejected.[7] In their work, significantly calm nobility changed to a mysterious drugged or drowsy lassitude, or gave place to neurotic tension. An ambiguous, over-refined seductiveness affected their picturing of ideal physical beauty, which was often elongated and elaborated to the point of caricature. Art bred with art, and as with in-breeding of animals, secured a

7   Clark, Sir Kenneth, *A Failure of Nerve*, text of H. R. Bickley Memorial Lecture (London, 1967).

selective emphasis of inherent characteristics. An extravagant, artificially cultivated elegance succeeded natural grace. Curious gymnastic contortions and strange balletic posturings were gradually evolved from the energetic movements which had swung the figures of Raphael and Michelangelo into positions displaying complete physical control. Such deliberate flouting of cherished principles can only be effective when those principles are familiar and understood. As it came to be appreciated that: 'there are certain things that are beautiful just because they are deformed and thus please by giving great displeasure'[8] so the play of bizarre fantasy was encouraged. Much inspiration was found in the elaborate works from the Northern Gothic tradition, while the pessimistic imagination so frequently evident in these met sympathetically with the loss of confidence in the South.

Almost all the great artists of the fifteenth century turned away at some point from the belief in human perfection, ideal proportion and rational space.[9]

The sunny blandness and smiling suavity of Raphael was clouded in his later works. During the 1520s, Michelangelo used the elements of architecture in a contradictory, even capricious manner. In various ways and for many reasons the firm conviction of the Renaissance was undermined, until by about 1530 bella maniera was widely triumphant. Decorative virtuosity was displayed for its own sake; subtle and accumulative reference was cultivated; ambiguity and ambivalence were encouraged; ingenuity and artifice were admired. All the arts of the Renaissance aspired to the rational clarity of architecture and the solidity of sculpture; and all the arts of the Baroque aimed at the fluidity of paint or the sensuality of clay. All the arts of the Mannerists adopted the refined brilliance of the goldsmith and the intricate workmanship of the jeweller.

To demonstrate some of the distinguishing marks of Mannerism, and the transitional character of every work of art, the Canning Jewel is a useful example. It is not inappropriate to consider it in relationship to painting or architecture, since it dates from a time when no clear distinctions were drawn between the fine and the decorative or applied arts. An object of exotic fantasy, it is elaborate, precious, minutely detailed and finely worked. The refinement of luxury is emphasized by the veiling of pure gold under a coating of enamel, and the use of gemstones simply as highlights to the composition. It is built from accumulated detail in what amounts to an earlier Gothic tradition, each part being as important as the whole. Perhaps inspired by Mantegna's engraving of battling sea-monsters, it has reference to the classical interests of the Renaissance, but the natural animal skull with which Mantegna armed his sea-creature has been transformed into a fantastically grotesque mask. At the centre of the jewel is a fabulous objet trouvé – the torso of the figure being suggested by a great blister-pearl which owes its beauty to its deformed and strange proportions. Yet this, the stimulus to the creation of the whole design, is itself baroque. It forms a mere detail in the composition but its quality of voluptuous plasticity was eventually to surpass in importance the highly-wrought filigree of its setting. So, frequently the incidental detail of

8 Calcagnini, Celio, epigram on the Discobolos, in *Mannerism*, by John Shearman (London, 1967).

9 Clark, Kenneth, op. cit.

one age is elevated to the prominence of a main theme for another.

Once a pattern of thought and interest has been established, by whatever varied influences, it tends to affect all the creative areas of life. Gardens of the sixteenth century reflected the attitudes to visual effects which have been seen at work within the limits of jewellery design. Directly descended from the medieval enclosed garden, they were generally small in scale, and isolated from the natural world by alleys of leaves, trained to form an architectural tunnel. The neat beds and paths were arranged in abstract patterns which could best be appreciated visually by standing on a terrace above rather than by walking among them. Once upon the paths, the pleasure of response to walking-out the pattern could be intellectually enjoyed. Nature had been tamed and trained to perform tricks for the pleasure of the onlooker, delighted no doubt by Man's cleverness as a teacher. The plants which filled the beds were chosen for their scent and for their decorative effect, but also because they were rare, new, strange or exotic, or because they had meaning from long traditional associations. The plants appealed emblematically, and could be *read*. Set among this artfully arranged nature, as focal points, were decorative devices – statues,

Sixteenth-century gardens were small in scale, and isolated from the natural world. They were best appreciated from a terrace above. (Douce prints.)

28

fountains, obelisks, each one prized as much for its ingenious references as for its individual design. The garden was a complex private pleasure for an intellectual élite.

By the late seventeenth century, the garden was enlarged in all directions, as much under the general influence of the expansive theatricalism of the Baroque spirit as under the specific influence of the French master gardener Le Nôtre. It became a group of many symmetrically arranged *parterres*, in which each single unit was itself clearly the descendant of the whole layout used during the sixteenth century. Multiplied in number and grouped in balanced order on each side of broad avenues, the *parterres* spread away through groves of clipped trees, as far as the eye could see. The small, private enclosed and decorative world had been thrown open to form a vast public setting for ceremonial promenades – no longer something for a select few, but for a huge, astonished assembly. The preference for immense, bold effects exciting an emotional response in the observer which had characterized Roman Baroque during the first half of the century was adapted in the second half to the needs of the French court. A national temperament, cooler, more logical than the Italian, retained the splendid scale and the theatricality, but imposed a firm, ceremonial discipline upon the arts. It was this French, classically orientated,

By the late seventeenth century, gardens had become much enlarged, under the expansive, dramatic influence of Baroque styling. (*Recuille des plus belles veües des maisons royales de France: Jardin de St. Germain en Laye* by G., N. and A. Perelle, late seventeenth century.)

Right
Certain aspects of Renaissance attitude and style are typified in this work, with its cool, considered intellectualism. (*The Triumph of Caesar* by A. Andreani after Mantegna's painting of 1486–92, the original being in the process of restoration.)

Below
Rubens' free adaptation of *The Triumph of Caesar*, executed early in the seventeenth century, displays all the pomp and excitement of Baroque styling. Its richness of colour is typical, and in complete contrast to Mantegna's work.

The Canning Jewel, made in Italy late in the sixteenth century, provides a perfect example of the way that age adapted the Renaissance style to its use. At the same time, its incidental detail offers inspiration for a later period to elevate into prominence. The designer seems to have fused together the opposed mermen in Mantegna's Renaissance engraving (*above*), producing a decorative Mannerist fantasy with a huge baroque pearl as its centre. It was the opulent plasticity characterizing such *objets trouvés* which would eventually surpass the filigreed ingenuity of its setting as a focus for interest. The carved ruby on the tail and cluster of pendant rubies are much later additions to the piece. (The Canning Jewel; *Battle of Sea Gods* by Andrea Mantegna, *c.* 1490.)

Reaction to planned formality is evident in this layout for one section of a garden. (Design by Batty Langley, depicted in *New Principles of Gardening*, 1728.)

Baroque which set the standards for Europe in the late seventeenth century.

However, a need for change began to be felt even at the heart of the machine after some thirty-five years of iron control. By 1728 the general reaction to planned formality is evident in a layout for one section of a garden in 'the New Style' from *New Principles of Gardening* by Batty Langley. The balanced *parterres* and the geometrical regularity were largely thrown aside. Paths wriggle haphazardly in pretty, serpentine curves. The senses are invited to run about, for the sheer fun of discovering in which unpredictable area the line will stop. Form is subordinate to decoration, which has been confined within an area suiting a domesticated human proportion. Such a garden is not natural – the informality is still artfully contrived, but that informality contains a *suggestion* of naturalism. The stiff grandeur has been softened into the picturesque and the pretty. Classical Baroque had evolved into Rococo. England, with its permanently romantic, naturalistic and informal preferences, was to make its greatest and most influential contribution to this international style through a new art of landscaping.

It is apparent from these few examples that a very wide field of reference must be employed to establish characteristics of expression. If the fashionable dress of any epoch displays similar, or comparable, characteristics to those observed in a varied selection of other contemporary works of art, then it is justifiable to claim that dress had its part in the total expression of an age. Superficial preference for a particular shape, form or line would not substantiate the claim; nor would mere similarity of motif used to decorate a dress, a chair or a cup. Evidence of a definable attitude to life, of a deliberate aesthetic, of marked social preferences and usage, must also be clear. It must be remembered that 'dress' has been used deliberately in a specific sense. Highly controversial aspects of decoration, involving the colouring or carving of the flesh, the attachment to the body of objects having strong symbolic association, or the wearing of skins or pelts in which the marked characteristics of the animal are purposely retained, belong to less well-defined areas, and fall outside the consideration of dress as a form of art. In the following pages the principal changes in fashionable dress during and after the Renaissance will be examined, with reference to the outline of stylistic developments described in this chapter.

I will heere huddle-up some few ancient fashions that I remember.

Michel de Montaigne
Essays, XLIX 'Of Ancient Customes'

Clothes make the man, but man makes his clothes

In order to appreciate fully the fundamental and expressive changes in dress which were brought about by new ideals and artistic attitudes evolved during the fourteenth century, some knowledge of the way European dress had developed before that time is essential. The origin of dress in the sense defined in the preceding chapters was dependent upon the invention of weaving, for it was only then that true creativity could transform the primitive methods of decorating the body. Once the use of the loom had been established – indicating a settling, if not settled, society – then one simple way to dress the human form was to swathe it in a rectangular length of fabric, taken more or less exactly as it was cut from the weaving frame. Unless an immense length of material is used (as in the still current instance of the sari) wrapping the body is a chancy business. Constant re-wrapping or adjustment is needed, because the fabric slips and shifts on the mobile figure. A more certain stability and composure can be achieved by tying or pinning the rectangular length. The limbs, having much greater flexibility than the solid mass of the torso, require freedom for their movement, and human ingenuity devised many different arrangements of the drapery which could bypass or accommodate the arms and legs.[1] Clothing of this temporary kind, either wrapped or pinned, formed for centuries the staple for Europeans. It is governed by certain principles. Truly 'weaver to wearer', it is the fabric which is of primary importance. Nothing at all needs to be done to the finished textile except by the person who wraps himself in it. When the garments are removed (for one layer may be wrapped or pinned over another) there is nothing to distinguish them from other woven rectangles, such as a bed-cover or a curtain (for which indeed they could readily serve should need arise). Even in wear, nothing fundamental to the clothing differentiates men from women, young from old, large from small. Under these circumstances the two distinct concepts of custom and fashion will, of necessity, be confined to colouring, surface patterning or incorporated decoration, and to the particular method of draping or pinning. Incidental details – the arrangement of the hair, the addition of separate

1 Practical diagrams of many such arrangements may be studied in:
Houston, Mary G., *Ancient Egyptian, Mespotamian and Persian Costume* (London, 1954).
Ancient Greek, Roman and Byzantine Costume and Decoration (London, 1947).
Broby-Johansen, R., *Body and Clothes* (London, 1968).

ornamental accessories or jewellery – may mark distinctions between the
sexes, the ages, or the individuals, but major differences are blurred into a
generalized appearance. Such dress tends inevitably towards the egali-
tarian, with the exception that its final effect must depend upon the skill
of the wearer. When the sight of the naked body was frankly accepted, if
clothes for any reason proved inconvenient or unsuitable to the moment,
they would be taken off, and if by chance they fell off, the revelation
occasioned neither undue surprise nor excitement. Clothes set off the
body, which was valued for its own perfections, and this individuality
could be revealed at will. Such rational, democratic, humanistic clothing
was significantly the dress of the Greek city states.

A simple way to anchor a length of fabric more securely to the person
is to pass the head through a slit cut in the centre of the rectangle. The
pendant flaps, falling at front and back, if permanently stitched to each
other, will encase the torso from armpit to hip, while allowing the arms
to emerge above and providing complete freedom for the movement of
the legs below.

To this simple form the refinements of extra narrow tubes, placed at
right-angles, may be added to cover the arms, and triangular-shaped
sections can be inserted into each side of the lower part, making the
garment widen towards its hem. This allows unrestricted leg movement

36

A length of fabric would be slit horizontally to allow it to be passed over the head, thus forming the basic tunic. Seamed beneath the arms, the garment was held in to the body by a belt. Extra rectangles were added at right-angles, to form sleeves.

The later structure of the tunic tended to concentrate the fullness at each side of the garment, even when held by a belt.

without any exposure of the limbs. For the first time, these additions necessitate cutting into laboriously produced rectangles of woven fabric but notably not in such a way that any is wasted. A further small refinement is the insertion of a square gusset below the armpit, when the sleeves are very narrow, to give a more graceful appearance and an increased ease of arm movement. Several such tunics may be worn one above another. If these are graduated in length, or the outer ones are left only partially stitched at the sides, it will be apparent to an observer how many are possessed. For still greater effect an extra unseamed length may be draped or pinned over all, combining the two distinct systems into a single ensemble.

Seamed garments must involve very different principles from those which apply to unseamed lengths. When not in wear, the tunic remains essentially a garment. When a shape, however simple, has been permanently imposed upon the fabric, it will suggest that it cannot readily be used for any other purpose than that for which it was clearly intended. On the other hand, since the shape approximates only vaguely to that of the body it has been constructed to conceal, the final or fashionable effect will depend far more upon how well the clothing is arranged and worn by its possessor than upon the work of the newly-introduced third party. Between the weaver and the wearer, the craftsman who stitches

To give a tighter fit, the tunic could be pulled in to the body by underarm lacing. Tightening both sides gives a more symmetrical and neater fit to the garment. There is some evidence to suggest that this method of fastening continued in use by both sexes until the seventeenth century. An example survives which belonged to Ferdinando de la Cerda of Spain, who died in 1211. This laces only on one side.

2 Lucie-Smith, Edward, *Eroticism in Western Art* (London, 1972).

the simple geometric sections together has intervened – but as yet he is a shadowy, unimportant figure. The completed tunic, permanently stitched, must be put on by pulling the entire garment over the head, so that it cannot be narrower anywhere than the width across the shoulders. This means that there is still little in the shaping to confine its use to one particular shape or size of body. Within reason, anyone can wear another's clothes. The important difference between such garments and those which are only draped or pinned is that they cannot fall off, nor can there be any unpremeditated exposure of either body or limbs. By allowing for the possibility of even violent energetic movement within the garment, its removal is seldom required. Significantly it was this tunic-form which was perfected and adopted throughout Europe during the early Christian period. A universal religion was adopted by a securely covered and universally dressed people almost unparticularized by either sex, age or oddity, in clothing. By their form such clothes tended to obliterate differences and cover deficiencies at a time when Man was unconcerned with 'miserable rather than glorious'[2] individual bodies in this world, and concentrated mainly upon what was to become of individual souls in the next. It is a simplification, but not an unhelpful or outrageous one to say that customary distinctions between leaders and led were made only by the use of sumptuous textiles and added precious ornament.

The decision to make clothes which would fit closely to the form of the body brought with it the first major step towards fashion in our presently accepted sense of that word. Contrary to majority opinion, my firm belief is that this step was taken by men rather than by women. Some form-fitting insulation between vulnerable flesh and the bruising hardness of metal armour must always have been a necessity. The great activity required in fighting would demand maximum unhampered movement. The desire for complete protection would suggest the maximum of covering yet the minimum of material. The resulting pared-down casing, worn without armour, presented a splendid new being, individually shaped, yet with all oddities of form smoothed away by a layer of firm padding. Women, seeing this new possibility, would eventually demand a personal adaptation from their tailors, when it must have become immediately evident that, not only were there many individuals of approximately similar shape, but that there were also two quite distinct sets of subtly differentiated form – those of men and women. Such an explanation seems to indicate at least in part a functional origin for fitted clothes.

Yet some abortive experiments to fit fashionable garments closely to the bodies of both men and women seem first to have been made during the twelfth century, at a time when there was a premature Renaissance. These experiments consisted generally (as far as can be deduced from unsatisfactory evidence) of dragging a too-small garment together by temporary underarm lacing, instead of permanent stitching. Less usually, a too-full garment was perhaps gathered over the torso; the gathers being drawn up and stitched on the right side in a honeycomb pattern, imparting a slight elasticity. The first successful development of *cutting-to-fit* occurred during the fourteenth century, when the lively stirrings of a more radical Renaissance began to be felt. Clothes then acquired ambiguity from a

desire to express opposing ideas. The Christian demands of modesty and the prudent concealment of the body were subtly combined with a reviving humanistic interest in physical display. Although the age was beginning to experience a passionate need for the revitalizing effects of principles native to the pagan Classical world, Christian tenets were never to be totally abandoned nor truly denied.[3]

Cutting and tailoring of great ingenuity were now rapidly evolved to perfect a new ideal, and the craft of making clothing moved through a series of developments more complex than any known before. Nothing since the introduction of the loom had had more far-reaching effects upon the appearance of the human race. The complementary roles of male and female – the active and the passive aspects of nature, either based upon biological function and temperamental differences, or upon centuries of conditioning – began to be more clearly divided and emphasized. The first serious signs of what was to become an almost complete separation appeared. As yet, however, Woman remained quite clearly Adam's Rib – a slight variation created from the same source – and the two sexes existed in a quiet harmony, visually at least, during the blissful freshness of the early Renaissance, evolving in the Late Gothic world.

These newer clothes were governed by yet another set of principles. The middle-man, the tailor, who made women's clothes as well as those for men, assumed an importance equal to that of the weaver and the wearer. Textiles themselves had now to be viewed in a rather different way. They were transmuted by the process of tailoring into an entity

3 For discussion of this matter see.

Seznec, J., *The Survival of the Pagan Gods* (New York, 1953). Wind, Edgar, *Pagan Mysteries in the Renaissance* (London, 1958).

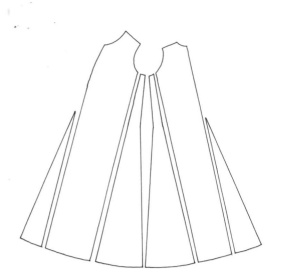

The construction of the robe from many individually shaped pieces assures the even distribution of fullness all round the body. (Garments using this system have been found at Herjolfnes, Greenland, dating from the late fourteenth century. They are now in the Danish National Museum, Copenhagen.)

The body of the doublet, made from four parts, gives close fit and accurate shaping.

The removal of excess fabric, horizontally as well as vertically, gives the eight-piece doublet more subtle shaping around the chest and hips, preventing wrinkling at the waistline.

which did not exist without it, and so had become raw material – only part of a whole. Sculptural form was given to the garments by the introduction of curved seams which enabled the fabric to lie smoothly around the supporting mass of the body. The individual shape of one particular person was thus necessarily built into the garment, remaining even when the garment was removed, as a reminder of the unique being for whom it had been created. It was no longer so easy to wear another's clothes. The impression of the wearer's person and personality remained increasingly a permanent feature of dress. Conversely, his physical appearance was assisted by the tailor, who could idealize the body, smoothing out the bumps and disguising the accidents of nature by judicious padding or controlling pressure. As bodies came back into minds, they did so with a subtle difference. Once, clothes had depended for their effect upon the body which they dressed; now, gradually, the body was to become dependent for its effect upon the clothes which gave it form.

In the efforts both to define and to idealize the body, many carefully shaped pieces were assembled together to make up each garment. First the tunic, originally formed from a single rectangle with the addition of two triangular gores at each side, was more carefully made from as many as twelve separate graduated pieces, so that if desired it could mould the torso from shoulder to hip, and then widen into a softly flexible bell. I propose, for simplicity, to refer to this type of garment, its upper part fastening either in front or on both sides from armpit to hip when closely fitted as: the gown. It appeared in many variations, but was essentially a robe widening from shoulder to hem, and hanging with the fullness

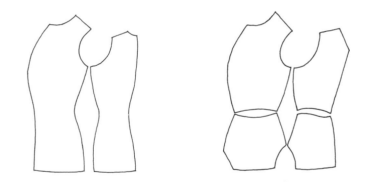

evenly disposed all round. This method of construction gave a far more refined effect than that of the earlier tunic form, in which all fullness was concentrated at the sides. The characteristic body covering for an active male was cut first from four separate curved pieces, seamed at shoulders, sides and back, and fastened down the front. Internally padded and quilted, it presented a smooth outer surface. Later, to assure even closer unwrinkling fit, it was made from eight shaped pieces, four above the waist and four below. (This will be termed: the doublet.) A little later still the female bodice and skirt were evolved, cut as separate entities (though stitched together), each having its own character: the bodice to shape closely, the skirt to gather fully about the figure. Thus again, two principles fused in one form. Every possible characteristic inherent in woven textiles was explored and exploited, including the use of the bias grain, which in the ever lengthening masculine hose would allow the fabric to cling like a second skin over the leg.

Quite as important at this time as the growing exploitation of sexual and other individual characteristics was the development of regional idiosyncrasy and interpretation of these basic themes. Under the pressure of new social stresses the unifying effects of one religion, one formal language, one social system and one form of dress were gradually disintegrating. Individuality of person was extended to include individuality of groups, towns and nations. While in Italy the strength of the early Classical tradition, with its emphasis on knowledge and observation continued to be evident in a reasonable, balanced style of dress, in which the natural dignity and proportion of the body was never totally eclipsed, in the North, fantasy and imagination were given free rein to produce dress which drew attention away from the body and on to itself. These clothes employed an exaggerated expressionism which seemed to increase the height and to attenuate the extremities of the person, so detracting from his apparent weight, mass and monumentality. Yet basically, cut and construction in both areas of Europe were derived from the same principles and employed similar forms and techniques, as late Gothic and early Renaissance ideas struggled for supremacy. Equally, cut and construction within those different areas were shared by both sexes, each using only the simplest variations on the same themes. Even in the details of headgear, this community of expression was frequently evident, and footwear was undifferentiated for men and women.

Not only changes of interest, philosophy and social structure affected dress. Since the twelfth century at least towns had been growing in size and importance throughout Europe, and courts, royal, princely or ducal, formed the gemstones held in this new urban framework. The essential setting for fashionable dress was provided by these centres for display and competitive emulation. In place of the customary dress which had simply set the privileged apart from the masses, the concept of fashionable dress now began to emerge. It called for constant change in an effort to keep a recognizable difference between one privileged individual aristocrat and another; and a still further difference between these, as a group, and the many prosperous individuals of the merchant class. As yet fashionable dress remained in all essentials public dress: bold, emphatic, theatrical; effective when viewed at a distance, and adding its splendour to the constant performance of ceremonial which maintained privileged existence.

Once the idea of cutting, shaping, padding and stiffening textiles to fit, improve or improvise upon the natural shape of the human body had taken hold, an instinctive impetus developed these principles to increasing extremes. Coincidentally the scientific exploration of the structure of the human form had become an interest for artists and scientists alike, focusing even more attention upon the body. The male frame, with its firm covering of muscle under a thin layer of flesh, its skeletal breadth of shoulder and volume of rib-cage, its narrow hips and long legs, began to be emphasized by padding above, and by closeness of fit below, until a man appeared an almost abstract form – an isosceles triangle standing on

The clothes are diffused, leading the eye into the air and on to the ground. The body of the wearer seems less important than the mass of the head-dress and the bulk of the train. (Detail from a French manuscript, c. 1465.)

Far right
These Italian clothes are compact, concentrated closely around the unified mass of the wearer, producing a sense of reasoned proportion and balance in the figure. (*Triumph of Venus* by Francesco del Cossa, c. 1465. Fresco in the Palazzo Schifanoia, Ferrara.)

its point. The lighter female skeleton, with its small thorax and broad pelvis, long torso and relatively short legs, all generously covered by soft malleable flesh, was eventually re-shaped by pressure above and distended by frames below, until a woman too became an abstract – a broad-based cone, exactly reversing the abstraction of the male.

By the 1540s, clothes were no longer simply moulded to the body or draped about it, but impressed it firmly, and encased it in a rigid abstract shell. The remoulding and remodelling, by padding, by pressure, by boning and by stiff understructures provided the basic principles upon which was built the costume I shall term Manneristic.

The fantasy and imagination of
Mannerism: a capital letter S.
(*Nova Alphati Effictio* by Theodor
de Dry, 1595.)

Mannerism

There is no excellent beauty that hath not some strangeness in the proportion.

Francis Bacon
Essays, XLIII 'Of Beauty'

The complex of attitudes and tendencies which are indicated by the stylistic term Mannerism (a selective term not applicable to all works produced during a specific period) seemed to move like a wave across Europe in the sixteenth century. Its visual beginnings are to be found in the work of some of the younger generation of Italian artists during the 1520s. By the thirties it had come to France, brought there in large measure by invited Italian craftsmen. The flood extended to all northern Europe, including England where it rose to a full surge after about 1560, then died away gradually again during the first twenty years of the seventeenth century. In Italy, Mannerism evolved from the indigenous Renaissance style, which had come under strong influences from the Gothic North during the first quarter of the sixteenth century.[1] As the wave flowed northward it met sympathetically with the surviving Gothic tradition, from which, gathering yet additional effects, it was further transformed from its original appearance.

The various garments which made up the masculine fashionable dress of the sixteenth century were themselves adaptations of the forms and types evolved in the medieval world, worn like the stratified layers of a geological specimen. Next to the skin was the shirt, descended from the simple ancient tunic, pulled on over the head. Above this came the doublet, adapted from the closely cut and wadded body-covering originating probably in the fourteenth century. By the late fifteenth century, the ever-increasing tightness and rigidity of this garment had begun to have a lasting effect on physical development, or at least

1   Clark, Kenneth, op. cit.

deportment. Leonardo da Vinci noted that for the study of graceful and elegant movements:

> you should select someone who is well grown, and who has not been brought up in doublets, and whose figure has not therefore lost its natural bearing.[2]

The legs were encased in long hose which by the mid-fifteenth century extended from foot to hip. By the end of the era, they reached as high as the waist, being joined together at the seat to form a single garment, the front opening covered by the movable gusset named the cod-piece. Cut from woven fabric with a single seam running up the back of each leg, the hose had their only freedom provided by the very slight elasticity which comes into play when the textile is placed on the limb with its warp and weft running diagonally across the vertical. Restrictive doublet and hose, being closely united to each other by a number of strings, or 'points', formed a combination into which the wearer was literally 'trussed'. Paradoxically, Renaissance physical display was provided only by the sacrifice of freedom. Over doublet and hose was worn the gown, another variation of an earlier type of garment, the gored tunic. Generally made now as an almost full circle, it flared out from the shoulders in springing, rounded, lively folds.

These are the basic elements upon which the appearance depended. Though many other garments could be worn in addition, all were variations upon one or other of these principal types. We may first concentrate upon one important item – the hose. The only illustrations which show hose untrussed and rolled down are needless to say all of separate hose, dating from before 1500, and are also needless to say always of working people. Their utilitarian stockings are shown as unlined, having only an internal facing of white linen, about two or three inches deep, at the top edge, to strengthen the working of the eyelet-holes for the 'points'. Fashionably they were worn always over lining socks or stockings. Andrew Boorde, physician to Henry VIII, recommended in his *Compendyous Regyment or a Dietary of Health* (1542):

> Let your hosen be brushed within and without and use linen socks, or linen hosen next your legs.

Putting on such unyielding dress must have been a strenuous business, and demanding the services of a page or valet on all occasions, if it was to look well. The servant was trained to 'strike up the hosen clean', that is, without a wrinkle; and William Harrison in the 1580s mentioned 'then must the long seams of our hose be set by a plumb-line'. About the turn of the fifteenth century, it became the fashion to make the hose from two or more different textiles, joined together most usually at the thigh. The parts were then referred to as upper- and nether-stocks, the nether-stocks covering the lower leg, while the upper-stocks, starting from knee or mid-thigh, rose to cover the groin and buttocks, but the separate sections were in principle (if not always in practice) stitched together to form a complete garment – long hose. Gradually the upper-stocks became the

2 Da Vinci, Leonardo, *Notebooks*, edited by Irma A. Richter (London, 1952).

Far left
Later development of the trunk-hose was indicated by 1500, in the embroidered decoration and slashing of the upper stocking. (Details based on two figures in *The Ordeal of Fire* by Giorgione, *c.* 1500, in the Uffizi Gallery, Florence.)

Upper-stocks gradually became the centre of attention around 1500. (Based on a figure in *The Adoration of the Magi* by the Antwerp Master, in the Groeninge Museum, Bruges.

centre of attention. Made either from patterned fabric, or embroidered or decorated with applied bands of braid, or strips of contrasting textile, they took on the appearance of diminutive, closely fitted shorts. As early as 1500, an alternative to applied decoration was provided by cutting vertical slits around the thigh of the hose, allowing the contrasting colour of a lining or an under-stocking to show through. An idea rapidly developed:

> . . . a paire of hose, upper stocked with carnacion-coloured satten, cutte and embrowdered with gold and also lyned with fyne white cloth.[3]

Before the middle of the century a new appearance had clarified. Elaborately patterned, slashed, and sometimes padded upper-stocks, were stitched at about mid-thigh to plain nether-stocks. At the same time the cod-piece ceased to be a simple triangular gusset and assumed prominence. Shaped into an abstraction of the male organ, it was rigidly padded, and the entire male population of Europe above the age of three appeared to be suffering a severe epidemic of priapism. The cod-piece served many arbitrary purposes. It had always been used as a convenient pocket for small articles, but a description of 1596 mentions that:

> His spectacles hang beating over his cod-piece like the flag in the top of a maypole.[4]

An even more general use for this padded projection was as a pincushion – pins being in constant demand for the nice adjustment of various parts of the costume. It would seem that this extraordinary display received a

3   Wardrobe Account of Henry VIII, 1536.

4   Lodge, Thomas, *Wits Miserie*, 1596.

All decoration of the upper-stocks, the cutting, 'pullings-out' and any padding was held close by a band at the groin in front, and stopped at the top of the hams behind, leaving the cheeks of the buttocks undistorted. By the 1560s, padding in general continued all round to waist level, and grew immensely in volume. (*Lower illustration*: detail from *Kunstbüchlin* by Jost Amman, 1578.)

quite casual acceptance. During the 1550s, all decoration of the upper-stocks, the cutting, the 'pullings-out' and any padding was held close by a band at the groin in front, and stopped at the top of the hams behind, leaving the cheeks of the buttock undistorted, their natural shape visible beneath the tautly stretched fabric. A late survival of this strange arrangement may be seen on a foreground figure on page twenty-eight. By the 1560s the padding was in general continued all round to waist-level, and grew immensely in volume, the trunk-hose swelling out into pumpkin-like forms, their outer layer being cut into or composed from long strips or 'panes'. These are *facts*; the development to this point seems plain and logical. But to see that an evolutionary process has taken place – to see how one step suggests inevitably the next – does not explain why a particular step was taken at a particular time, or why a development was made in one direction rather than another. This is indeed the style of dress for an age, but how does it relate to the wider general style of the age itself?

Before considering this point fully it will be useful to examine the next developments in this type of clothing. So far each stage has been plain to see, but during the sixties, and onwards to the end of the century, the situation became more complicated. There was an outburst of invention and innovation, a wild exuberance of variety. In Germany the paning and 'pullings-out' of the trunk-hose had been carried to an extreme, and the 'Allemagne' fashion soon spread beyond its native area. The excessively full linings ballooned and drooped into immense bags, hanging sometimes well below the knee, or at other times, although shorter, they were gathered into double-decker puffings. The cod-piece was at its most enormous, its decoration at its most emphatic. (Significantly the Germanic temperament seems to run to extremes of expression. In Germany the Gothic style was given its most frenetic architectural and sculptured statement; there too the Rococo reached the highest peak of asymmetrical fantasy; in the Germanic areas Neo-classicism was found at its most pedantically austere; and there also the movement now named Expressionist had its beginnings.) Throughout Europe in the 1560s and 1570s there appeared newer forms of leg-covering to take their place beside the old. These were true breeches, made with seams on the inside and outside of each leg, and depending from the waist instead of rising from the feet. These so-called 'Venetians' were fastened to the doublet by the old system of 'points'. They took many varied forms: skin-tight; a smoothly padded inverted pear-shape; a fully gathered or pleated construction, distended by a hip-pad worn inside; or else made to hang wide and free, like loose 'Bermuda' shorts. Finishing just below the knee, they were all worn with separate (now knitted) stockings supported by garters instead of being joined to the breeches to form a single garment. There was more variety still. From the 1570s onwards, trunk-hose were at times so diminished that they rested as a mere skimpy padded roll decorating the hip-bones, and so were worn of necessity in conjunction with either long-hose of the late Gothic type, or over knee-breeches of the 'Venetian' kind. Alternatively, the hiatus between the top of the newly fashionable knitted stockings and the base of the full old fashioned padded trunk-hose was covered by 'canions'. These separate extension-tubes were stitched into

Panings and 'pullings-out' in Germany were carried to ridiculous extremes, and the 'Allemagne' fashion soon spread to other countries. (Detail from *Kunstbüchlin* by Jost Amman, 1578.)

True breeches, the so-called 'Venetians', were fastened by the old-fashioned system of points, in the 1560s and 1570s. (Detail from *Kunstbüchlin* by Jost Amman, 1578.)

The figure at the far left wears long-hose, together with trunk-hose reduced to a hip-roll. The others wear 'Venetians' and stockings. The figure at the far right wears the hip-roll over 'Venetians'.
(Details from the *Judgement of Solomon* cushion at Hardwick Hall, Derby.)

Right
The man wears trunk-hose with 'canions', while the costume of the female figure is a mixture of fact and fantasy. (Detail from *The Garden of Pleasure* by J. Saenredam, *c.* 1605.)

the breeches' mouth, the lower edge being either tucked into or left to fall over the top of the stocking. On occasion 'canions' were made from a textile of a different colour and patterning from either trunk-hose or stockings, so that the disintegration of the parts was emphasized.

For about twenty-five years variations on any of these different leg coverings appeared fashionably together in all areas of Europe. There was no real unity of theme:

> But now there is such a confuse mingle mangle of apparell . . . and such preposterous excesse thereof, as everyone is permitted to flaunt it out in what apparell he lusteth himself, or can get by any kinde of meanes.[5]

The picture is confusing as at no other time until quite recent years. Invention and ingenuity were much prized, and the Mannerist appreciation of variety was certainly well catered for in masculine leg-wear.

> The need for variety is a very human one, in almost every period and society. It is the exaggerated pursuit of variety . . . that is so essential a feature in the cultural background of Mannerism.[6]

The hose, one link with the Gothic past, formed the basis for a typically Mannerist expression. The doublet, also inherited from that earlier age, formed another.

An essential feature of the doublet was its wadded interior. Except for a narrow panel down the centre-back it was usually padded and quilted throughout, the facing fabric then being laid separately over this interlining to give a smooth unwrinkled exterior. Already by the 1530s the fashionable man displayed an exaggeration of physical attributes which

5 Stubbes, Philip, *Anatomie of Abuses*, 1585.

6 Shearman, John, *Mannerism* (London, 1967).

Sua ceteruni in
Sponsi, quinque autem
eis erant prudentes et
quinque fatua qua erant
...a ..imeti
lampadibus suis
non ceperant oleum
fecum, prudentes vero

Interior of a doublet, late
sixteenth or early seventeenth
century. The fabric is black
figured velvet, lined with yellow
silk. The eyelet holes for trussing
the points have been covered at a
later date by a band with metal
rings, to which the breeches
would be hooked.

far exceeded the bounds of Renaissance moderation, dignity and grace.
His firmly modelled doublet helped an abstracted ideal. He appeared
broad-shouldered and barrel-chested, while a proudly displayed virility
between his legs projected forcefully through the skirts of his jerkin. Over
all, the swinging fullness of the puffed-sleeved gown added to the effect of
bulky swagger. Between 1536 and 1541 Michelangelo was painting his
Last Judgment on the end wall of the Sistine Chapel in Rome. Was it
coincidence alone, or some community of spirit that accounts for the fact
that while those vast muscular colossi were being created, an aggressive
masculinity was also evident in fashionable European dress? Those massive
figures, which are the culmination in exaggeration of a Renaissance ideal,
feature in a 'doom-painting' – a Gothic theme rarely employed in Italy
before this time. They are an end and a beginning, for it was against the
later work of Michelangelo, as well as of Raphael and Leonardo, that
the younger generation seemed to react, while developing from it the
exaggerated elegance and strangeness seen in the contemporaneous work
of Parmigianino, Primaticcio and Bronzino. Mannerism was one curious
issue of the 'Grand Manner'.

By the late 1540s the doublet was considerably lengthened, though still
bulky. Its apparent waist dropped almost to the groin, while the broad
sleeves and wide collar of the gown were much reduced in volume. The
whole figure grew slimmer and less heavy, but was still unequivocally
masculine. During the next decade, however, as the trunk-hose were
gradually inflated towards a characteristic onion-shaped form, the doublet
changed again. The waist level returned to normal at back and sides but
dipped sharply to a point in front. During the sixties, the fronts of the
doublet from breast-bone to belly acquired additional stiffening from
paste-board, glued canvas, whalebone strips or some similar system. At
each side of the front waist an internal loop was stitched, through which a

The full, puff-sleeved gown
added to the effect of bulky
swagger in the 1530s. (Henry
VIII and his father from a
cartoon for the lost fresco in
Whitehall by Hans Holbein.)

cord was passed, to be tied tightly before the front of the doublet was fastened. This not only held the garment close in to the small of the back and the sides of the rib-cage, emphasizing a narrow waist, but helped the stiff front edges to stand out in a sharp ridge, like the breastbone of a trussed fowl. In profile the hard edge took on the outline of the base of a pea-pod. By the 1580s high fashion had exaggerated this feature into a massive, stuffed and pendulous paunch. 'Hard-quilted', the peascod-belly drooped often to the fork. This caricature of portly middle-age, appearing above the youthful slenderness of long legs elegantly displayed in un-wrinkled hose, is equivocal, and provides a blatant contradiction of that ideal physical perfection which the Renaissance had prescribed. Such developments are clearly seen in the other arts of the period. Painters had deliberately contradicted by surreal fantasy and impossible juxtaposition the rational suggestion of place, space and proportion, only achieved such a short time before. Michelangelo and Giulio Romano played whimsical games with all the established rules of classical architecture. Benvenuto Cellini and Giovanni Bologna had smoothed and elongated bodies and limbs into impossible boneless elegance, twisting their sculptured figures into balletic serpentine poses in which former force and virility were transformed into airy lightness and artificial grace. With these changes in mind, it would be strange to find the real beings of the era left mundane and unaltered. The contradiction of youth and age together in one person, the oddity of proportion resulting from the weight of the body, and the fragility of the legs emerging below the absurdity of the shrunken trunk-hose, may surely be counted an equivalent expression in dress to the experiments in painting, architecture and sculpture which contradicted, exaggerated or deformed established practices. At no other time in the history of Western fashion has a distended belly been artificially suggested rather than corrected or disguised. There must be some explanation for the fact that a physical feature at such odds with any normal majority view of attraction should have been worn with pride for about ten years. If such a feature *had* attraction, the appeal was surely not directly physical. As an expression of one aspect of Mannerism it appears at least accountable.

The Mannerists loved ambiguity as well as contrariety. In the portrait of Lord Leicester, from about 1570, doublet and hose are again in the full service of typically Mannerist expression. The wasp-waist and broadly rounded hips give to the dashingly masculine Earl a very feminine form. Comparison between this portrait and that of Henry VIII is instructive. Again, for almost the only time in the history of fashion, an exaggeration of certain physically feminine characteristics was used in male costume. To make confusion worse, it was the fashion for men to wear a beard. On the other hand, it should be remembered that at the same time the female bodice was cut often without any shaping for the breasts, making it almost identical in form to the masculine doublet:

> The women also have . . . dublettes and jerkins, as men have . . .
> buttoned up the breast, and made with winges, weltes, and pinions
> on the shoulder poyntes, as mannes apparel is, for all the world.[7]

Watching a play by Shakespeare it is impossible for us to experience the

Overleaf
At no other time has a distended belly been artificially suggested, rather than corrected or disguised. (*Left: The Banner Bearer* and *Right: A Pike-Man* by Hendrik Goltzius, 1587.)

7   Stubbes, Philip, op. cit.

A°87

57

full Mannerist relish with which at least the intelligentsia in a contemporary audience must have watched a boy playing a girl disguised as a boy. We believe that they missed something of the illusion of reality. Perhaps we miss something of their formal mental gymnastics. The arts of the age are filled with epicene figures. The painted or carved females seem boyish; their breasts artificially applied. The males are willowy and smoothly unmuscled. Similar ambiguity appears in written description:

Sick-thoughted Venus makes amain unto him
And like a bold-fac'd suitor gins to woo him.

'Thrice-fairer than myself;' thus she began,
'The fields chief flower, sweet above compare
Stain to all nymphs, more lovely than a man,
More white and red than doves or roses are;'

. . . He burns with bashful shame; she with her tears
Doth quench the maiden burning of his cheeks.[8]

Hercules and Omphale was a favourite theme. The hero sat spinning among the women while for love he had sacrificed his club and lion-skin to deck the heroine. These things may be the exploitation of eroticism of a highly sophisticated kind. But they are also symbolic of the reconciliation of opposites in harmony; of the active interacting with the passive. All the visual and literary creations of this age tended to the symbolic, the allegorical, the emblematic, and require reading with the intellect as well as enjoyment by the eye. Sense is as important as are the senses.[9] Clothes are not likely to have been excluded when all else was so affected.

One important item of dress, shared by men and women alike, was the ruff or 'band'. Developed quite logically from the natural frill into which the fullness of the shirt or shift would fall when gathered into a neck-band, it was formalized during the 1550s. Eventually it was detached, and grew in width and depth, reaching to a maximum after about 1580. Then (stiffly starched and 'under-propped' by wire or paste-board 'supportases') each flute of fullness was separately shaped with a specially designed hot iron and neatly pinned to form a regular series of figure-of-eight 'sets'. This complicated piece of artifice effectively divorced the head from its body, presenting it as though in isolation, and thus played a part in the technique of disintegration which marked the age in many other ways. Hugely distended sleeves, another bisexual feature of the last two decades of the century, quite as effectively separated the arms from the trunk; their division emphasized by a decorated wing or welt jutting out from the armhole. The exact equality of consideration given to each part of the body suggests that the whole was conceived as an accumulation of the parts, as opposed to an entity in which the parts depend upon the whole. Such an attitude of aggregation is evident in the architecture, art and literature produced by the late Gothic world. Later Mannerist dependence upon this attitude, particularly in England, is emphasized by the quite conscious Gothic revival here at the end of the sixteenth century. Spencer's homage to Chaucer; the medievalism of Sidney's *Arcadia*; the detailed preciousness of the miniaturist Hilliard's illumination technique; the

8 Shakespeare, William, *Venus and Adonis*, 1593.

9 *For discussion of these matters see*:

Wingfield-Digby, George, *Elizabethan Embroidery* (London, 1963).
Girouard, Mark, *Robert Smythson* (London, 1966).
Strong, Roy, *The English Icon* (London, 1969).

renewed interest in the ritual splendour of the tournament, and the Gothicism displayed in many of the 'paper-work' prodigy houses, bear witness that such ideas did affect all the arts,[10] and should consequently be sought also in the field of dress. Even if they do not always bear the easily recognizable marks of direct Gothic imitation, this should not blind us to the possibility of their influential presence. The jewel-like quality of Gothic work, the high finish which results from self-absorbed concentration upon discipline and detail, is to be found once again in the complexity and preciousness of Mannerism. In dress the rich encrustation of the surface, which was kept within the bound of the whole composition during the fifties and sixties, had broken out into a riot of cluttering detail by the eighties. The textiles which composed the garments were almost destroyed by cutting, stamping, punching or drawing-out many of the very threads that wove them. They were obscured by embroidery, braiding and appliqué, and were then (in feminine dress) often veiled under 'cypress' or other transparent fabrics, themselves also cut, drawn or decorated in ways similar to the textiles they shaded. A grid-like dimensionality which allowed layer on layer to be seen through slits cut into one surface, upon which another had been built-up, was then further crowded by ornamental additions. Bosses and buttons marked intersections or were placed in interstices formed by the trimming. Every part of the figure was hung about with chains and pendants. They dangled from hair, ears, neck, wrists, biceps, elbows and waists. Brooches were pinned on ruffs, veils, sleeves and hats, as well as on to doublets and bodices, in an unmatched display. The complex surfaces of the already decorated dress became a field for extra ornament – a veritable 'paradise of dainty devices', as a poetry anthology published in 1576 was entitled. For this age, enough seems never to have been sufficient. There had always to be another meaning, another use, another possibility, another probability below and above the surface. Dress formed a decorative visual equivalent for the way in which words were used. Through the surface meaning, another meaning was intended – just as in the pictorial representation of physical beings there was invariably reference to qualities, circumstances or analogies, symbolically or emblematically revealed. Unity was given to all this diversity in dress by colour and counterchange. In a portrait of Richard Sackville[11] his white doublet is patterned with embroidered honeysuckle flowers in black and gold; his black trunk-hose are powdered with the same motif in gold outline only, while in between, the fabric is cut to reveal a white lining; white stockings, supported by black garters fringed with gold lace, are themselves embroidered with black and gold; and the black and gold flowers of the doublet are then reproduced on the white shoes, which fasten with roses of black lace, spattered with golden spangles. Over his shoulder a black cloak, braided with gold, reveals a lining of 'shag' in which loops of black and gold unite in equality. Colour holds all in harmony; pattern is made to counterchange like a musical theme. 'Shag', a high piled looped fabric, artificially suggests fur. 'The fancy outworks nature'[12] in every way. Significantly the cuts were seldom neatened, their edges being left raw. This rough detail makes an effectively casual contrast to the high degree of finish all around, giving a slightly temporary look to something clearly built to last. The cuts, by being

10 Buxton, John, *Elizabethan Taste* (London, 1963).

11 *See the Catalogue of the exhibition 'The Elizabethan Image', Tate Gallery, 1970.*

12 Shakespeare, William, *Anthony and Cleopatra*, 1606–7.

Lord Leicester in the high fashion of the late 1560s. A wasp waist and swelling hips give a feminine appearance contradicted by the beard. (*Left: Robert Dudley, Earl of Leicester* by an unknown artist, c. 1565.)

The abstraction of the torso by pressure appeared in combination with dragging medieval skirts at a time when Mannerist principles were emerging. (*Right: An Englishwoman* by Hans Holbein, 1527.)

arranged in deliberate patterns, counteract the insolent extravagance of slashing expensive fabric, yet add the further insolence of declining to finish the effect, which could make it seem too intentional.

As early as the 1520s, the tendency to alter the soft surface of the female body by pressure had become evident in the dress of women. By placing seams far to the side of the bodice, running straight down from the front of the armpit to the waist, the fabric of the front section was stretched taut across the breasts, so that instead of shaping the garment to fit around them they were suppressed by it and forced upwards towards the clavicles. As yet the heavy volume of the skirt hung in medieval folds about the

The soft torso of the female form was transformed into a rigid cone, inverted above another to epitomize the deliberate eccentricity of Mannerism. (*Left: Lady Jane Grey* by an unknown artist, c. 1550. *Right: Lady in Court Dress* by Nicholas Hilliard, c. 1585.)

legs so that their motion would be apparent in walking, in spite of the
mass of fabric carried over them. But in Spain (as subject to fantasy and
expressionism as the countries of northern Europe), during the second
half of the fifteenth century, a system by which the skirt was supported on
a series of graduated hoops of cane had introduced a greater abstraction
to the entire figure. The adoption of this regional idiosyncrasy by the
circles of high fashion outside Spain seems to have been made by way of
masquing costume or fancy-dress. Hoops are mentioned in this con-
nection as an exotic novelty at the English court in 1519.[13] The widespread use of this Spanish innovation during the sixteenth century has
been credited to the political, military and economic importance which
the country then acquired, and in particular to the many expedient
marriages and other contacts made with European courts. On the other
hand, it must be admitted that a significant expression will generally be
contributed by individuals or groups displaying unusual vitality, and that
as increased vitality may mean political, military or economic development, it may also prompt idealistic and artistic development. Of course
vitality attracts attention and rouses response. The important definitive

13 Hall's *Chronicles,* 1519.

statement of abstraction, in which the soft torso was forced into a rigid cone, inverted above another, seemingly as rigid, which concealed the legs, suggests a motionless counterpart to the aggressively active masculinity so apparent during the 1540s and 1550s. However, as masculine dress gradually developed those ambiguous effects already discussed, so the dress of women was subtly modified towards a similarly ambivalent statement. While remaining recognizably and essentially feminine, the man-tailored garments employed the bi-sexual ruff and sleeves, the doublet-like bodice, epicene hat and shoes, and identical textiles, trimming and ornamentation. Under such circumstances a new dimension is added to Queen Elizabeth I's statement, 'I know I have the Body but of a weak and feeble Woman, but I have the Heart and Stomach of a King'. The concepts of aggregation and the reconciliation of opposites, so much employed in figures of speech, and in allegorical pictures at this time, were just as essential in female dress as in contemporary male costume. During the last thirty years of the sixteenth century the various under-structures distending the skirt (itself often trussed to the bodice by points) provided comparable variety of shape to that found in masculine leg covering. Various intermediate, rather round-hipped bell-like forms were derived from the sharply sloping cone of the Spanish farthingale. These were contemporaneous with bolster shaped pads or 'bum-rolls', carrying the skirt out horizontally at hip level and then allowing it to drop straight to the ground. It was not in variety, abstraction and ambiguity alone that Manneristic expression was most evident in late sixteenth-century female dress, but in a deformity analogous to that of the masculine 'peascod-belly'. The Mannerist artist was not expected to imitate nature in what he represented, but to imitate nature only in the way in which he too was inventive.

Whoever adds strangeness here and there to his style, Gives life, force and spirit to his paintings.[14]

Fancy was expected to surpass nature herself in the production of the extraordinary, an aim surely affecting the tailor of women's dress as much as other artists. One characteristic high-fashion of the 1590s, carried to an extreme at the English court, obliterated the female body as completely as had Gothic fashions, but not by Gothic form or style. The torso was flattened and elongated so that the waist appeared to be lowered almost to the fork; the width across the hip was carried to grotesque extreme by the flat-topped farthingale. This round or oval frame was tipped forward, its front edge falling almost to knee-level, while the skirt supported by it was shortened to clear the ground by several inches. The result was a complete caricature of the long-bodied, wide-hipped, short-legged structure to which the female form naturally tends, but all suggestion of feminine softness or voluptuousness was completely denied by the sharp, angular, brittle appearance of the whole. Deformed and strange, it could surely only have pleased by giving great displeasure.

. . . the grotesque is only a way of expressing in a tangible manner, of making us perceive physically the paradoxical, the form of the unformed.[15]

Intermediate, round-hipped, bell-like forms, were derived from the sharply sloping cone of the Spanish farthingale. (*Elizabeth I* by Crispin Van der Passe, 1596.)

14 Epitaph of Piero di Cosimo, 1521, quoted by Shearman, John, op. cit.

15 Durrenmatt, Friedrich, quoted by Toby Cole in *Playwrights on Playwriting* (London, 1960).

By the 1590s, the extreme high fashion of the English court liked to obliterate the female body by flattening the torso and elongating it so that the waist seemed lowered to the fork, while the width across the hips was carried to grotesque extremes. (*Elizabeth I* by Crispin Van der Passe after a drawing by Isaac Oliver, 1603.)

It must be confessed that dress of this type (as exemplified by late portraits of Elizabeth I) is a gift to those Freud-inspired commentators in search of the sexually symbolic. It requires little imagination to see that the costume in the illustration opposite transformed the Queen into a walking surrealistic fantasy, composed entirely of blatantly suggestive breast, buttock and phallic symbols. In a recent study, *Eroticism in Western Art*, Edward Lucie-Smith has commented on the great outburst of erotic energy which overturned High Renaissance ideals, and led to the triumph of Mannerism, and certainly there is apparent in all Mannerist art an incredibly inventive erotic ingenuity. This quality is usually cooled by its very intellectualism as well as by the jewel-like hardness of technique. Suppressing the real at the expense of the symbolic it is cerebral lechery of a special and sophisticated variety. Comparison between works by Correggio (who is never claimed as a Mannerist) and any by his contemporaries Parmigianino or Bronzino (who are), will prove that the latter appeal to the senses only in an indirect and complicated way. If then the costume in question is seen to be symbolically suggestive of sexuality as well as of majesty, it enforces rather than invalidates my contention that it is a characteristic expression of its age. Elizabeth's claim to be both feeble woman and mighty king would be emphasized by the inclusion of the symbols of both masculinity and femininity in the composition of one person. Even without the revelations of Freud such ingenuity of explanation would have been well within the grasp of any true Mannerist.

Fashionable clothing for both men and women between 1560 and 1625 displayed very markedly many of the characteristics which have been used to define the concept of Mannerism in the other arts. Such clothes were not merely ambiguous, epicene, beautifully ugly and strangely beautiful; they provided the wearer with yet another possibility. The overcoming of difficulty with panache was a point of honour for these stylists. In the impossible contortions into which Bronzino wove his allegorical figures there is no hint of strain or discomfort; no implication that the precarious balance, crammed so tightly into the confines of the pictorial area, could not be held elegantly for ever. They appear as unruffled acrobats performing incredible feats without any display of unease. To move well and to look right in the accumulated difficulty of late sixteenth- and early seventeenth-century dress must have required all that exhibitionism of a gymnast, who appears to make no undue effort. Every step, every successful movement, demanded the round of admiring applause which also greeted the tossing-off of a well turned sonnet; the delivery of a fine piece of extemporary Latin rhetoric; or the faultless taking of a part in some ingeniously woven madrigal. Such clothes were excessively difficult to 'get up' and keep in good order, as well as being difficult to put on and adjust. Although the basic form was built firmly into them, much of their effectiveness depended upon ephemeral arrangements, dextrously made with pins or laces during the process of dressing. All these things required great energy, firm discipline, highly skilled assistance and fine performance.

Mannerism, according to definition, is subjective, creating from the mind rather than from observation. For inspiration it looks to art rather than to reality. It is fastidious, depending upon cultural knowledge as

66

much as on direct experience. It is frigid yet erotic. It is artificial, ingenious, intellectual. Exclusive and aristocratic, it is private and provocative. Manner is of equal importance to matter and matter may well be employed as mere excuse for manner. It delights in the combination of contrasts: in variety and monotony; abundance and brevity; beauty and monstrosity; clarity and obscurity.[16] Closer examination of the costumes discussed can only amplify their qualification to be seen as a true and important expression of all the interests of their time, and to be a triumph of Mannerist style.

Bronzino's allegorical figures seem capable of impossible contortions, with no strain or discomfort; overcoming such difficulties with panache was a typically Mannerist point of pride. (*Venus, Cupid, Folly and Time* by Bronzino, *c.* 1546.)

16   Shearman, John, op. cit.

The two faces of Baroque

All our reasoning comes down to surrendering to feeling.

Blaise Pascal
Pensées

The peoples over whom we reign, being unable to apprehend the basic reality of things, usually derive their opinions from what they can see with their eyes.

Louis XIV

Certain effects and characteristics of Mannerism continued evident until 1625, or even longer, but the principle style which dominated in the first half of the seventeenth century was that conveniently to be distinguished as Roman Baroque. Developed, like the Mannerism with which it overlapped, from the arts of the High Renaissance, it shared identical sources in the work of Leonardo, Raphael and Michelangelo, but used them for very different ends:

> The deliberate eccentricity of Mannerism had removed art, tightly constricted by rules and prohibitions, from the experience of ordinary people. . . . Revitalization of the arts depended on the removal of the barriers between the world of the senses and that of the spirit, the renewal of contact between art and nature.[1]

With great virtuosity some artists of the young generation of the 1520s had inverted or perverted their inspiration. By fragmentation, abstraction and attenuation they had created the delicate, emasculated, intellectual complexity discussed in the last chapter. But another young generation, born after 1550, was maturing towards the end of the century, and together with artists younger still, was able to discover different

1 Sewter, A. C., *Baroque and Rococo Art* (London, 1972).

71

The architecture of Baroque
Rome is grand, bold and full of
movement, overwhelming
judgement with direct appeal to
the eye. (Basilica Vaticana from
Roma Moderna, 1741. The
church, begun by Michelangelo
in 1547 was completed in 1605;
the piazza was added in
1657–66 by Bernini.)

2   Studiolo of Francesco I de
Medici, Palazzo Vecchio,
Florence, designed by Giorgio
Vasari, 1570–2.

possibilities within the same sources by looking back through what was
disliked. In conscious opposition to an enervated preciousness, the new
expression ignored the pessimistic agony and neurosis undoubtedly
present in the works of the great men, noting there instead the force and
energy, the splendour and nobility, and above all the natural emotion of
which Mannerists had so disapproved. For the new men, size, weight,
grandeur, dynamic movement and bold modelling of solid plastic masses
emphatically defined by strong light and deep shadow, were the things
that mattered, and which they found had been to some extent expressed
earlier. Intensification and concentration were now required. For them
the importance of line must give place to that of form. Hard, enamel-like,
or curiously 'shot' colours were changed for those which were mellowed
and richly sensuous. The small, secret, sealed study without windows[2]
(erratically lit by candles whose flames gave glittering life to the massed,
minutely detailed treasures commissioned to please an individual whim),
had ceased to fascinate. Instead, vast public places, thronged from morning
to night with hoards of excited people avid for spectacular display,
proclaimed a different disposition.

At first the new art, synchronizing with the Counter Reformation, was placed at the disposal of the Church to assist the reassertion of her splendour and attraction before the eyes of an astonished congregation. During the second half of the century it was transferred, much modified, to the services of a divinely appointed monarchy.

The many great churches which rose in Rome around the middle of the century exemplify characteristics exploited generally by the style. Grand, bold, large, they seem full of movement and overwhelm mental judgement with direct appeals to the eye. Their walls sway often into sweeping curves, convex and concave, or are thrown into a rhythm of deeply contrasted projection and recession. Colossal orders leap up to the top of a façade, emphasizing towering height. Heavy mouldings jut out, and niches are deeply scooped in, adding to the richness of the field for the play of light and shadow, which, moving over the surfaces, changes emphasis from moment to moment. The rolling scrolls of volutes and consols organically fuse together the static geometry of rectangular constructions, and the immobile circle is compressed or pulled into a more dynamic ellipse. Steps with wide curving treads and shallow risers sweep down to meet the spectator, and projecting wings or colonnades, alternating sun and shadow, swing energetically forward like arms extended in an embrace. Doors and windows appear to be pierced through forceful sculptured cartouches, these stone surrounds seeming squeezed and moulded like damp malleable clay into serpentine dimensionality. Clustering along parapets and crowding on to ledges, ecstatic saints in billowing robes strain up and out, about to be carried into space by the explosive force within them. Inside the buildings, dimensional modelling blends with illusionistic painting to dissolve walls and ceilings into piled-up cloud-scapes, swarming with a riot of flying, trumpet-blowing angels; and openings are generously swagged with curtains deceptively carved from multi-coloured marble asymmetrically looped up with cords of gilded bronze. Sun pours down from small concealed windows to spotlight a thrilling moment of rapture held in the set-piece of a sculptural tableau. Excited, dramatic, theatrical, the appeal is uncomplicated and direct – particularly when augmented by the balletic ceremonial of gorgeously robed priests and acolytes, seen through the haze of incense, and accompanied by the ringing music of orchestras and choirs placed on all sides of the auditors to bathe them in waves of sound.

A painting by Caravaggio, one of the formative generation which forged the Baroque in the last years of the sixteenth century, serves to remind us not only that the style concentrates upon dramatic essentials, ignoring or softening irrelevant detail, but that it also views humanity with an eye to natural proportion. Here are no attenuated, over-beautified limbs, no boneless fingers bending into elegant serpentine curves, but instead, full, solid, weighty beings. Here is ordinary warm flesh and blood, not alabaster bodies with teeth of pearl and hair like golden wire. Living, breathing people, often coarse, seized at a moment of high intensity, are draped in supple yielding textiles instead of being cased in thickly encrusted, brittle shells. The theatricality is firmly rooted in spontaneous action and human emotion. It is not an intellectual pageant icily performed by abstracted mannequins.

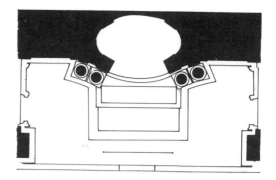

The theatrical concept, in which the ecstasy of St Teresa is set on a stage observed from side boxes, is here very apparent. (Plan of Cornara Chapel, Santa Maria della Vittoria in Rome by Bernini, 1645–52.)

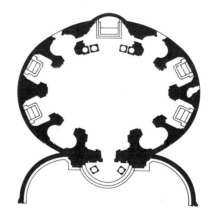

An example of Baroque plasticity. (Plan of Sant'Andrea al Quirinale in Rome by Bernini, 1658–70.)

Baroque styling often concentrates on dramatic essentials, softening irrelevant detail. (*The Supper at Emmaus* by Caravaggio, *c.* 1597–1600.)

In dress at this time, it is essential to discover similar interests, parallel expressions, like appearances, before it too may be claimed as Baroque, and already, at least by 1610, there is much evidence of changing taste to be found, suggesting such a development. The human body was beginning to be less confined and contorted. A more natural appearance was to be restored. The rigidity was softening.

The inflexible padding of men's trunk-hose (if these were still worn) was with increasing frequency discontinued, even by the 1590s. Only a thick, blanket-like interlining was used to round out the fabric, giving it weight and volume. The old-fashioned longitudinal cuts (the panings) gave place to deeply wadded pleats as the newer interest put modelling before line. The deforming belly disappeared before the new century, and the front edge of the shorter waisted doublet no longer projected in a sharp ridge. It tended to be concave rather than convex. The high stiff cylindrical collar of this garment still generally encircled the neck, but from its upper edge, an unstarched ruff, or 'falling-band', unsupported by wire, dropped down naturally to the shoulder, making a steeply sloping transition from head to trunk.

As the century wore on, the decorative border of many overlapping tabs which had trimmed the waistline of the doublet was increased in length while the girdlestead was raised. The now larger tabs were reduced in number; from as many as ten, to eight, and eventually to four. The resulting simpler doublet-skirts which fused gently with the body of the garment, instead of standing smartly out to mark its ending, now softened the break between the upper and lower parts of the body. By the 1620s, breeches of the 'Venetian' type, very variable in shape and fullness, but always unpadded, had fashionably replaced all forms of trunk-hose. Each of these adjustments combined together to give an effect of greater unity to the figure than had been usual for many years. In addition hair had been allowed to grow long, falling naturally on to the shoulders to emphasize that fusion of head and body which the falling-band had already suggested. The eye could glide over the whole person without being compelled to consider his parts.

Although the deep front point of the doublet, which rested on the stomach, was still to some extent stiffened to keep it in good shape, the entire garment was less closely fitted. To ease it further, long cuts were frequently made down breast, back and the upper section of the sleeve. A possibility of greater freedom of movement for the body coincided with an interest in the illusion of movement in architecture, painting and sculpture.

Between 1625 and 1630 (the years when the full effects of Roman Baroque were reaching towards a culmination in the other arts) that last remnant of the late Gothic heritage in dress, the doublet (which by its very nature tended towards rigidity and formality however much the spirit of a new age might modify it), although still worn, became less evident. It was hidden increasingly by a cloak slung about the body in an asymmetrical whirl of rolling folds, or it was covered by a loose *casaque*. This travelling garment, which had sleeves of a sort, might also be worn draped across the body by the ultra-fashionable, rather than put on as its construction suggested that it should be. The breeches, softly pleated now into unwadded folds, appeared beneath these enveloping wraps, but the legs were then swallowed up by the gaping mouths of the boots. These were made with 'bucket-tops', providing ample funnels to accommodate the fullness of the breeches when the boots were pulled up to their full thigh-height for riding. In general, however, they were pushed down to wrinkle into undulating creases below the knee; the wide, loose tops flopping about the lower leg. Deep flounces of heavy Flemish lace, or thick swaying fringes lolled over the tops of the boots. These were the trimmings of the spreading upper edges of the boot-hose – over-stockings of linen – intended to protect the finer silken hose from the grease and oil with which the leather was treated to keep it supple. This utilitarian excuse for an elaborate decorative effect was augmented by opulent scarf-like garters, which spilled loose bows with yet more lace-edged ends to dangle about the legs. The instep was covered by a huge curving butterfly-shaped spur-leather, projecting well beyond the width of the foot, and much larger than practicality could possibly require. The now freely flowing hair (or occasionally, apparently, 'perfumed perrukes, or periwigs, to show us that lost hair may be had again for money')[3] was crowned by a

3 Peacham, Henry, *Truth of Our Times*, 1638.

75

hat of which the generously sweeping, softly rolling brim was overlaid by full-length ostrich plumes to curl about its edge.

While Baroque effect is no doubt emphasized, even exaggerated, by the artist's personal style, in engravings by Callot or Bosse for example, nevertheless the basis in actuality is evident. The Frenchman, Callot, had worked in Italy between 1608 and 1621, returning then to France to combine in his pictures of costume the richness of Roman Baroque with French *chic* and panache in matters of dress, creating illustrations which epitomize the clothing of the High Baroque. Bosse was the son of a tailor, from whom perhaps he had inherited a sensitivity to clothes which prompted his production of figures displaying much elegance and grace, strengthened by a confident opulence. From the work of these two men it is clear that a quite new effect was the aim in dress. Old forms had been modified by new ideas to meet a changed mood.

To complement and assist the modifications to *form* there were other

Between 1625 and 1630, the doublet became less evident; the last vestige of late Gothic heritage was increasingly hidden in a copious cloak. (p. 76: from *La Noblesse* by Jacques Callot, 1629. p. 77: from *Le jardin de la noblesse française* by Abraham Bosse after J. de St Igny, 1629.)

changes. Textiles were less stiffened by quilting or multiple linings, their suppleness and lustrous satiny surfaces being left to make their own effect as light slipped over them, allowing luminous shadows to glow in the depths of the folds. If decorated by cuts, these were now very small, producing texture rather than pattern, and only spattering the shining silk with tiny specks of dark, sometimes interspersed with glittering spangles. The marking out of sections, seams and edges by lines of contrasting braid was much less usual. Braids were often matched in colour to the cloth to be less noticeable, or they were so closely ranged together, that again they provided texture instead of definition, and gave only the appearance of a finely striped, encrusted weave.[4] Embroidery, too, if used, employed small-scale patterns, very closely packed, to spread a dense network over the entire surface:

> I could accuse the gaiety of your wardrobe
> And prodigal embroideries, under which
> Rich satins, plushes, cloth of silver dare
> Not show their own complexions.[5]

In other words, however treated, the tendency of decoration was towards totality of effect.

4 *See* Portrait of Henry Rich, School of Daniel Mytens, *c.* 1640. London National Portrait Gallery.

5 Shirley, James, *The Lady of Pleasure*, acted 1635; printed 1637.

In masculine wear the supple undulation of leather, from thickest buff to finest Spanish, from heavily matt to smoothly glossed, had an important part to play in combination with the textures of pliant satins, velvets and closely woven woollen cloth. Equally supple were the favoured laces so liberally used. In complete contrast to the very fine 'spider-work' of Italy and Flanders which, stiffly starched, had made a spiky delicately linear edging to sixteenth-century ruffs and cuffs, the newer laces, whether needlepoint or bobbin, were much more rich and boldly worked. Built up in plastic dimensionality and opulently scrolling patterns, unstarched and exploiting the natural weight of linen thread, they drooped and draped, flopping about the shoulders and wrists and over the tops of boots. All things worked together towards new ends.

Just over a century earlier Castiglione's *The Book of the Courtier* had appeared. Published in 1528, it was based on a draft made between 1508 and 1516 during the years of the High Renaissance. Then, moderation, intelligence and the nobility of Man were emphasized in everything:

> to let you know what I think is important when it comes to the way
> one should dress let me add that I should like our courtier always
> to appear neat and refined and to observe a certain modest elegance
> though he should avoid being effeminate or foppish in his attire and
> not exaggerate one feature more than another.

A very different attitude is indicated in a scene from James Shirley's play *The Lady of Pleasure* first performed in 1635. Transformed by new clothes, Frederick, a young scholar, is instructed by a more fashionable friend.

Littleworth   Your French tailor
    Has made you a perfect gentleman. I may
    Converse now with you and preserve my credit.
    D'ye find no alteration in your body
    With these new clothes?

Frederick   My body alter'd? No.

Littleworth   You are not yet in fashion then. That must
    Have a new motion, garb, and posture too,
    Or all your pride is cast away. It is not
    The cut of your apparel makes a gallant,
    But the geometrical wearing of your clothes.

Steward   Master Littleworth tells you right; you wear your hat
    Too like a citizen.

Littleworth   'Tis like a midwife;
    Place it with best advantage of your hair.
    Is half your feather moulted? This does make
    No show: it should spread over, like a canopy;
    Your hot-rein'd monsieur wears it for a shade
    And cooler to his back. Your doublet must
    Be more unbutton'd hereabouts; you'll not
    Be sloven else . . .

Your doublet and your breeches must be allow'd
No private meeting here. Your cloak's too long;
It reaches to your buttock, and doth smell
Too much of Spanish gravity; the fashion
Is to wear nothing but a cape. A coat
May be allow'd a covering for one elbow, . . .

Satirical exaggeration is no doubt present but clearly breeches and doublet were, fashionably, no longer tied together by points, or even united by hooks and eyes, being allowed 'no private meeting'. A *mouvementé* negligence was the order of the day, and France, no longer Italy or Spain, was the arbiter of elegance. During the 1640s that casual but calculated grace reached its apogee and began an inevitable decline towards caricature, in which inherent slovenliness played an increasingly evident part. The most perfect fashion always contains the seeds of its own destruction.

The doublet shrank upwards from the waist, to become, in final decrepitude, a skimpy bolero, its short sleeves sometimes cut entirely into narrow ribbons. The breeches, resting loosely on the hip-bones, widened at the hems, first to a moderately tubular form, and then further increasing in volume, developed by 1660 into immensely full 'petticoat-breeches', looking often like a generously pleated skirt. Between the two, the shirt bloused boldly into public view. Since hooks and eyes took over their utilitarian office, the 'points', those narrow laces which once functionally tied the garments together had been transformed for more than a generation into a border of decorative ribbon bows around the waist. Now transferred from doublet-waist to breeches-band these useless ribbons formed a thick fringing of close-set dangling loops all round. Ribbon loops continued, often in broad panels down the outside seams, and closely edged the hem of each leg just below the knee. Several hundred yards of ribbon were required to trim a fashionable suit. Under the breeches full lining drawers were worn, gathered closely into the knee and finished there with deep valances called 'canons', frequently trimmed with lace. Emerging from the wide mouths of the breeches the canons hung around the lower leg to below the calf. They could be in two or three layers, and were sometimes starched to 'resemble paper lanterns'.[6] With the exposed shirt-sleeves often tied by ribbons into a series of lateral ballooning puffs, and periwigs continually increasing in length and volume to hang in great frizzy clumps on each side of the face, it seems no exaggeration that a man should 'look and waddle (with all those gewgaw ribbons) like a great fat slovenly water dog'.[7] When seen in action, such clothes must have provided an exaggerated visual expression of the Baroque interest in animated, bold theatricality.

At this time the clothes of fashionable women were still the product of the male tailor, and many parallels continued in the dress of the two sexes, but from the early years of the seventeenth century certain specifically feminine characteristics were exploited by Baroque style. The first two decades were a time of adjustment to a new ideal, a struggle for supremacy between the opposing motivations of Mannerism and of its energetic rival expression. Inevitably in the personal field of dress many individual preferences, for or against, provide muddling and contradictory examples,

By 1660, the breeches developed into immensely full 'petticoat breeches', often looking like a generously pleated skirt. (From *Divers costumes français du règne de Louis XIV* by Sebastien le Clerc, late seventeenth, early eighteenth century.)

6 *Les Loix de la Galanterie*, 1644.

7 Wycherley, William, *The Gentleman Dancing Master*, 1661–2.

79

After 1600, women must have changed with relief from the suppressing bodice of formal dress, into the unstiffened, short-waisted, domestically produced jacket. The illustration (*right*) is one of pink silk, embroidered with blue couched silk-cord.

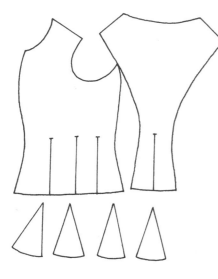

Far right
A fine example of Baroque rotundity in the female form, clearly showing that the hermaphrodite fixation of the Mannerist styling has passed. (*Lady Elizabeth Grey, Countess of Kent* by Paul Van Somer, *c.* 1610–15.)

but there was a growing tendency towards a different appearance. The immensely long, suppressing bodice of 1600 was probably only ever used for fully formal wear, and women must have changed with relief into the simple unstiffened short-waisted domestically produced jacket-bodices of which so many have survived. Constructed on a very ancient system in which the lower part was widened by the insertion of small triangular gores into slits made all round below the waistline, these bodices fitted neatly over skirts distended about the hips by the thick bum-roll. As the waistline of the male doublet shortened (and consequently widened where

An open-fronted gown worn
over the dress and surmounted
by a wired veil emphasizes
Baroque interest in mass. (From
La noblesse française à l'église by
Abraham Bosse, 1629.)

A further roundness began to appear in the inflation of the sleeves. A Baroque effect was achieved, with surviving sixteenth-century forms. (From *La Noblesse* by Jacques Callot.)

it encircled the rib-cage) so the bodice of a woman's formal dress was similarly adapted. This development brought female formal and informal clothing towards a greater equality of appearance, and the jacket-bodice began to be more generally worn on public occasions. The high, less constricted waist, in conjunction with a smaller hip-roll, gave a gradual transition from bodice to skirt. This was in complete contrast to the formerly sharply marked division between the long narrow torso and the wide framed-out farthingale. Parallel with developments in male dress, the move was towards greater freedom, unity of form, and a more natural proportion. Mass was emphasized at the expense of line. The neckline of the shorter, less deforming bodices, was cut often quite alarmingly low. High and close to the nape behind, it was scooped down in front into a deep round *décolletage* leaving the breasts almost completely exposed. Freed from suppression the bosom bulged sensuously in natural softness. The pneumatic modelling which was captivating architects, sculptors and painters was here exploited spontaneously by fashion, though an early hesitancy resulted in the odd combination of the falling-band worn above the exposed chest. Fully rounded forms were emphasized throughout the composition: in the ruff, in the dressing of the hair, the bared breasts, the line of the *décolletage*, the padded hips, and the deep funnel-shaped cuffs, which, retreating up the arm, revealed yet more softly rounded flesh. Women were undoubted women. The hermaphrodite fixation of the Mannerists had passed. Over such dress an open-fronted gown was still usually worn. Laid in small box pleats beneath the arms and across the back, the fabric fell to the floor, expanding over the hip-pad to give a very bulky appearance particularly when viewed from the rear. This gown was now often draped asymmetrically by drawing one front edge up towards the opposite hip, creating a number of obliquely curving folds among which light and shade could play.[8] Sometimes the gown was replaced by a diagonal drapery, passing under one arm and caught up in a knot on the opposite shoulder.[9] This was perhaps inspired by 'antique' dresses used for the masques which played such a prominent part at the courts of the age. Whatever the source it gave a distinctly fanciful air, and proves an interest in theatricality as an accepted part of daily life for the fashionable.

The Mannerist mania for excessive variety was also passing away rapidly by 1620. It had been formerly evident in the combination of bodice, petticoat and gown each of a differently patterned and decorated fabric.[10] The newer liking for a simple unity was established by having all three garments made *en suite*. From this time too a further roundness began to appear in the inflation of the sleeves. At first stuffed with bombast, they were later simply fully gathered into unstiffened but buoyant puffs, ending just below the elbow to expose the roundness of plump and dimpled arms. In painting, the smooth, firm, slim epicene adolescence of Bronzino's chilling Venus is a world away from the ripe quivering voluptuousness of Rubens' favourite models. There was a distinct effect of weight in the fashionable appearance – a slack, mature adiposity. This characteristic was produced by the exploitation, rather than the counter-action, of the sagging drag of inertia inherent in heavy fabrics. Conversely, in spite of the equal weight of late sixteenth-century dress, it conveyed no suggestion of heaviness. Rather, the smoothing effect of padding, and the taut distention over frames gave an impression of weightlessness – tense, athletic and youthfully muscular. In the seventeenth century the sensuousness of flesh had its counterpart in the rippling luxury of thick satin, simply cut and falling in full, generous, rounded folds. Satin, like flesh itself, invites the caress of the hand, and a most natural gesture sweeps to the side the front breadths of the skirt, breaking the vertical folds into swinging undulations, catching light and suggesting movement as the fabric is drawn back against the legs. This is the typical pose so

8 *See* Portrait of Lady Cary, *c.* 1614 ('The Elizabethan Image', Tate Gallery, 1970).

9 Portrait of Frances Howard, Duchess of Richmond, 1611 (The Viscount Cowdray).

10 Portrait of Lady Scudamore (Tate Gallery).

The Bohemian artist, Wenzel
Hollar, drew clothes reflecting
the new, fuller look, even
capturing the way in which
ladies bunched up full skirts
when walking, thus
unconsciously echoing the
exuberant ballooning of drapery
admired by artists like Bernini
in Rome. (From *Ornatus
Muliebris Anglicanus* or *The
Several Habits of English Women*,
published in 1640.)

From the 1660s onwards spontaneity was discouraged, while rules and regulations multiplied in the field of etiquette and ceremonial. This engraving embodies formality. (By Juan Dolivar after a design by Jean Bérain, late seventeenth, early eighteenth century.)

elegantly portrayed by the painter Van Dyke, who was in England by 1632 to record the dress of the smart set about the court. In the engravings of a lesser artist than Van Dyke, working in England around 1640, there is proof that the Flemish painter's pictures do not show a merely personal studio confection. The Bohemian Wenzel Hollar drew similar clothes similarly worn. He caught the characteristic manner of bunching up the skirt when walking, to emphasize that exuberant ballooning drapery so beloved of artists like Bernini far away in Rome. Such a gesture was surely not accidental, but the unconscious spirit of an age working to achieve a recognizable style in every aspect of life.

Such clothes are instantly acceptable. Simple, easily appreciated, they require no intellectual interpreting. Complementing rather than obscuring the human form, they are as expressive of the spirit of Baroque as any work by Borromini, Bernini, Rubens or Rembrandt. That style was shared equally by fashionable men and women, who despite the many differences between them, still shared certain of the incidental items of dress as well as its general effect. Textiles, trimmings, hats, collars, gloves, muffs, stockings and shoes were almost interchangeable and had as yet no specific customary or associative connotations to limit their use to either one sex or the other. Often, until mid-century, the bodice of a woman's dress might be made also in almost exact imitation of the man's fashionable doublet, and it was known by that name. But already there were indications of another change. The vitality of Italy was in decline. Although there the effects of the High Baroque would continue well into the eighteenth century, her power as a generator of new ideals was passing. Spain had withdrawn into an aloof and ritualistic conservatism, holding a dead hand coldly over widely-scattered European possessions. Another focal point was needed. France had been gaining in political, economic and artistic importance, under the influence of Cardinal Richelieu from 1624 until his death in 1642. A renewed energy was evidently there. The essential spirit of drama, theatricality and emotionalism, which had produced Roman Baroque was gradually channelled into a new direction by the different needs of another national temperament. It did not disappear but was adapted to suit an outlook predominantly clear and logical. In 1661, after the death of the protector Cardinal Mazarin, the young Louis XIV came into his own and a new machine moved into conscious motion. Art was to be used towards the glorification of a divinely appointed king and the enrichment of a nation whose carefully nurtured luxury industries were to become the envy of all Europe. A significant indication of the future is provided by French reaction to an Italian artist whose work epitomizes the concept of High Baroque. The great Gian Lorenzo Bernini was summoned to Paris in 1665 to design a new façade for the old palace of the Louvre. His several projects did not please: they were too demonstrative, too dramatic; although classically based they were insufficiently restrained. In 1667, the cool severity of Perrault's disciplined classical design was approved instead, and when Bernini's long-expected, exuberant equestrian statue of the king at last arrived in France in 1684 it was relegated to a seldom visited corner in the park at Versailles.[11] By that date the small brick hunting lodge built for Louis XIII had been almost totally enveloped by the pompous yet barrack-like

11 Hibbard, H., *Bernini* (London, 1965).

From 1662, the styling of the coat became noticeably smoother. A long-waisted look became popular, often with pockets set vertically to increase the illusion of slenderness in the silhouette. (*Left: Habit d'Espée* and *Right: Officier du Roy* by Jean de St Jean, *c.* 1685.)

palace which exists today. The Salon de la Guerre was already open, the Galérie des Glaces was nearly ready. Versailles had become the centre of fashionable Europe. A new pattern had been set. The effects of spontaneity were discouraged, and rules and regulations multiplied. Etiquette ramified and ceremonial flourished. The palace was crowded with courtiers and thronged by the public. Every moment of the day provided a grand theatrical ritual led by the king, symbolized as the Sun. He rose when his bed curtains were publicly opened in the morning, and set when they were publicly closed at night. Such things are not themselves the

Far left
Portrait of a gentleman in black, by Terborch, *c.* 1660: the doublet, petticoat-breeches, canons and cape are Baroque elements already given a formality in the manner of wearing. Although the colours are dark, they have a sombre richness, typical of the period: compare with page 30.

One remaining symptom of high Baroque vigour appeared in the design of shoes; with high, thick, block-like heels, and an opulent curve to the instep, they were squared off at the toe both horizontally and vertically.
(*Left: Homme de qualité en habit galonné* by St Jean, 1693.
Right: Homme de qualité en habit de Teckeli by St Jean, 1694.)

cause of a changing attitude, but rather are they symptoms of it. So it is with dress.

When the doublet had begun to shrink into a useless mockery of all former intention during the 1650s, it was increasingly covered by a coat or *casaque* correctly worn on the body, with the arms put through the sleeves. This coat was very loose at first, but once adopted for formal wear, it was smartened up and made to fit. In fashionable circles from about 1662, it began to extinguish the Baroque exuberance of the billowing shirt and swinging fullness of beribboned petticoat breeches as these disappeared within its confines. Cut to an ever closer fit, it smoothly covered the body from shoulder to knee by the 1670s. 'It makes me show long-waisted, and I think slender'[12] was the fashionable boast. To prevent any break in this elongated line the pockets were cut vertically; or if made horizontally were placed quite impractically low; '. . . it can never be too low . . . the pocket becomes no part of the body but the knee'.[13] The elaborate decoration and undisciplined fullness of the breeches died away gradually

12   Etherege, George, *The Man of Mode*, licensed 1676.

13   Vanbrugh, John, *Virtue in Danger*, acted 1696.

93

and they were made to fit neatly. Often the tiny doublet (now serving the purpose of a waistcoat) was replaced by a vest, which was constructed exactly like the coat. The front edges of both garments were decorated for their full length with precise symmetrical rows of lateral embroidery or braid, to mark the buttons and buttonholes. A uniform regularity governed the whole and all its parts.

> The courtier formerly wore his own hair, dressed in doublet and breeches, flaunted broad lace ruffles and was a free-thinker. This is no longer the thing; he wears a wig, a close-fitting coat, plain stockings, and he is devout; fashion decides it all.[14]

Some hint of former ebullience was still preserved in the increasing volume of the full-bottomed peruke, dressed by the 1690s into towering twin peaks and falling in profuse curls on breast and back. A belated symptom of untamed Baroque vigour appeared too in the design of shoes. Equipped with very high, thick, block-like heels which compelled an opulent curve to the instep, they were finished forcefully by squaring off the toes both horizontally and vertically. These massively architectural, heavily-built accessories provided one of the most distinctive features in the dress of the final decade of the seventeenth century. When worn they would have assured an exaggeratedly strutting deportment fully expressive of the pompous grandeur which marked every aspect of the court of the Sun King.

At about the same time that the miniscule doublet was being relegated to a subordinate role beneath the coat, changes appeared in the bodice of the woman's dress. A small interlining, stiffened across the back and down the sides by strips of whalebone, had always been built into the short bodies of formal dresses during the 1630s, to counteract in practice their apparent freedom. This encouraged upright carriage and provided support to raise the breasts into the prominence so essential to the full expression of the age. During the 1650s the number of bones was gradually increased, the bodice was lengthened again, and its *décolletage* widened to allow the shoulders to emerge. Before 1660 the sleeve was set in as low as the deltoid muscle on the upper arm. This, together with the placing of the shoulder seam at a very oblique angle, far back on the trapezius, greatly emphasized the natural sloping transition from the neck into the body. It also reinstated a restriction of movement.

> I remember there was a Fashion not many years since, for Women in their Apparel to be so Pent up by the Straitness and Stiffness of the Gown-Shoulder-Sleeves, that they could not so much as Scratch Their Heads . . . nor Elevate their arms scarcely . . .[15]

The front of the bodice, dropping into a deep point towards the belly, assumed a shallow concave curve from there to the middle of the breast-bone. Its renewed closeness of fit forced the breasts upwards to bulge out above the almost horizontal oval of the neckline. By 1660 the formal bodice had become virtually a corset. From that time much straighter, this 'whale-bone body' had upwards of forty stiffening strips incorporated

14 La Bruyère, *Characters*, 1688, translated by Jean Stewart (London, 1970).

15 Mace, Thomas, *Musick's Monument*, 1676.

By 1660, the formal bodice had
virtually become a corset.
(English ivory knife-handle,
c. 1660.)

between its double interlining. The extra rigidity of an unyielding horn
busk ran the full length of the front from the *décolletage* to the extreme
depth of the point, where it was tied into place by a busk lace. The long
trained skirt, open in front for formal wear, was caught back by jewelled
clasps or neat symmetrical knots of ribbon into a series of puffs, exposing
the petticoat. This was generally laid out in a regular geometric pattern
formed by broad bands of metallic lace, interspersed with rows of flat
galloon (a narrow braid). As the man's coat tightened into a slimming
disciplined uniform so the woman's formal dress imposed a new inflexi-
bility eminently suited to the court parade.

Complementary to the higher dressing of the male periwig, women's
hair was also gradually raised in front, and by the last decade of the
century was overtopped by the wired-up frills of the small lace cap which
had usually covered the back hair for twenty years. This towering
'fontange',

which makes a woman's head the basis for a many-storied edifice,
the order and structure of which vary according to her whims,[16]

16   La Bruyère, op. cit.

95

was further augmented by standing loops of stiffened ribbon. In addition
to this formal but totally feminine decoration a woman's shoe now
differed markedly from that of a man. A long vamp curved over an
instep thrown into prominence by a very high heel, but set well forward
towards the centre of the foot, the heel was not a solid-looking block. It
curved emphatically away from a wide top into a narrow waist and out
again to a small base. The toes, though horizontally squared off, were not
vertically blocked-up into a box-like finish, but narrowed to form a thin,
flat, spatulate tip.

The fashionable dress of both men and women in the second half of the
seventeenth century interpreted the regimented ceremonial, the disciplined
restraint and the academic precision of French modifications of an earlier
exuberant Baroque. It also introduced a far more definite distinction
between the appearance of the two sexes than had ever been evident
before. Dress, although so clearly an essential ingredient of period style,
possesses its own particular dynamic. Here it is necessary to mention two
other points related to the specialized development of clothing because of
the effects these had on later stylistic expression. Firstly, there is evidence
that seasonal changes dictated by physical convenience began to receive
some fashionable notice during the seventeenth century. For example,

Complementary to the men's
high periwig, women's hair was
gradually raised in front, and by
the last decade of the seventeenth
century was overtopped by frills
of lace, wired up. (By Robert
Bonnart, c. 1690.)

Jean de la Bruyère noted in *Characters*, published in 1688 that:

> he is dressed simply but comfortably, I mean in some very light
> material in summer and something soft and warm in winter.

From fashion plates of about this date it is clear that winter dress was often
trimmed with fur, not so much for the actual comfort this would give as
for the soft warmth it could suggest. Conversely, from *The Man of Mode*
(1676), a play by George Etherege, we learn that while *point d'Espaigne* is
not so rich as *point de Venise* it 'looks cooler and is more proper for the
season'. The idea of physical comfort was apparently both symbolically
implied and even receiving a little practical consideration. Majesty was no
longer to be the single aim of dress. A new possibility of adding further
justifiable variety to display was opening up. Secondly, the creators of
fashionable clothes were beginning to emerge from the shadows as
identifiable beings whose personality could be imposed upon the dress
they made for others to wear. The wearer began to share the credit for his
appearance with an artist whose individuality might eclipse his own. Yet
the wearer basked in a reflected glory by advertising his individual judgement as a client. In the past *all* credit was given to the patron. In the
seventeenth century we hear more of the patronized. From Mme de
Sévigné there is word of the incredible work of the tailor Langlée;
Molière had mentioned Perdigeon; and Etherege catalogues the 'most
famous hands' in Paris who had created the 'slight suit' in which Sir
Fopling Flutter made his sensational arrival in London: 'The suit – Barroy;
the garniture – Le Gras; the shoes – Piccar; the periwig – Chedreux.'
(It should be noted that in spite of the praise given to the *cut* of the coat,
the *garniture* by Le Gras receives an equal credit.)

While fashionable clothes were thus helping to express the spirit of an
age, a new ethic was concurrently developing by which they would be
governed.

Men's shoes were bolder, and
thicker in proportions. These are
maroon leather with black heels,
dating from the late seventeenth
or early eighteenth century.

Men's and women's shoes were
sharply differentiated: the
female version has a long vamp,
and is carried on a high heel.
These are cream leather, with
red braid trimming.

Rococo design for a panel by
Jeremy Wachsmuth (1711–71).

Rococo

If you should see your mistress at a coronation dragging her peacock's train, with all her state and insolence about her, 'twou'd strike 'you with all the awful thoughts that heav'n itself could pretend to from you; whereas I turn the whole matter into a jest, and suppose her strutting in the self-same stately manner, with nothing on her but her stays and scanty quilted petticoat.

Sir John Vanbrugh
The Provok'd Wife 1697

The metaphysical poets of the seventeenth century and the psychologists of the twentieth seem to be at one in their attempts to understand the strange ambivalence of Man who so constantly turns in revulsion against all he has most desired.

> Oh wearisome Condition of Humanity!
> Borne under one Law, to another bound;
> Vainely begot, and yet forbidden vanity,
> Created sick, commanded to be sound;
> What meaneth Nature by these diverse Lawes?
> Passion and Reason, self-division cause.[1]

What later appear as the opposite emotions of protective love and destructive hate may be by no means simple representations of two externally opposing groups of instincts. To a great extent they may originate in one confused and violent desire which is inherently unstable because in its very greed it threatens to destroy what it would most ardently preserve.[2]

Considered in this complicated context it soon becomes evident that 'the

1 Greville, Fulke, *Chorus Sacerdotum*, added at close of his neo-Senecan drama, *Mustapha*, 1609.

2 Money-Kyrle, R. E., 'On the views of Melanie Klein', in *Psychoanalysis and Politics* (London, 1951).

swinging pendulum of taste' is a too simple symbol. While oscillation from one extreme to its opposite is taking place vertically, a slow, laborious movement is being made horizontally. Although the long confining coat of the late seventeenth century brought men back to a uniform formality after the relative freedom of the middle years, the total restriction of Gothic doublet and hose was never reinstated. For every two steps forward, only one is taken back again.

In France, national temperament, individual personality and political expediency had combined together to restrain the more volatile aspects of Southern Baroque, while retaining its force, boldness and grandeur. Its impressive majesty and assertive solemnity were exploited in the service of the French monarchy, which required also a strong measure of discipline, as well as subservience. Rotund fluidity and emphasis were brought to order, marshalled, drilled, and set to perform spectacular balletic manoeuvres in neatly balanced, rigidly defined compartments. Such ideas were clearly expressed, as has been shown, even in garden design, where the exuberance of nature was forced into an expansive but tightly controlled decoration – rich but predictable, grand but obedient.

Even kings, though divinely appointed to their office, eventually grow tired of it, and long to escape – to become entirely human. In 1699, Louis XIV was getting old and bored by all the splendour he had created. When designs were submitted to him for the redecorations at the tiny Château de la Ménagerie he wrote a famous minute which marks the first real crack in an apparently unchippable glaze. The building was in preparation for the reception of a girl of thirteen who would become the Duchess of Burgundy. The schemes of the court designer had naturally employed the expected standard classical formula – marble, gilt bronze, and solemn, painted scenes of gods, goddesses and allegorical figures, all in richly sonorous colour. The king, who had been captivated by the charm and vivacity of the young Duchess-to-be, saw that such a setting must prove unsuitable to her personality. 'It seems to me', he wrote, 'that something ought to be changed as the subjects are too serious; a youthful note ought to appear in whatever is done. You will bring me some drawings, or at least some sketches. There must be an air of childhood everywhere'. New designs were made by a younger artist which were approved – and the Rococo had officially begun. In 1701, redecorations were carried out yet again at the great main palace. In the anteroom to the king's bedchamber, instead of the prescribed parade of classically draped deities marching round the cove, there is a gaily dancing troupe of golden children, carrying garlands of flowers, against a background of dainty trelliswork. From this time on the rigid formality began visibly to dissolve.[3] In Largillière's portrait of the king and his family, painted in 1710,[4] Louis and his son continue to cling to earlier convention, even defiantly exaggerating the immense mass of the wig in a grand climactic gesture, but his grandson, the young Duke of Burgundy, has noticeably modified the quantity of his hair, tossing shorter curls carelessly back from his face. On the wall behind the group there is a filigreed lightness of gilt decoration, in which the geometric sharpness at the corners of the panelling is softened by an inward turn. A ginger-jar and a basket of fruit are casually grouped at one end of a great consol table, replacing the usual

3 *See* Kimball, Fiske, *The Creation of the Rococo* (Philadelphia Museum of Art, 1943).

4 Wallace Collection, London.

formality of a symmetrical *garniture*. In 1715 the old king died, leaving a baby, his great-grandson, as an heir, and his brother, the Duke of Orléans, as Regent. The relief of this release from an iron grip which had been held for half a century was marked by the retreat of the court from the monstrous megalomaniac inflation of Versailles, back to the urbane intimacy of Paris. This briefly is the factual background which serves much too simply to emphasize another general tendency to change. Such changes are not the prerogative of kings and courts, who are themselves only a part of a more continuous major human experiment. When men gave up doublet and hose in favour of coat, waistcoat and breeches they had taken an irreversible step towards the modern world, in which technology, science and industry take precedence over instinct, intuition and craftsmanship. Some yet deeper mysterious instinct seems to have suggested, however, that a balance must be kept between the rational and the irrational; and between the adventure of experiment and the safety of familiarity. It was this secret sense, perhaps, which had suggested an intensification of the apparent differences in the roles of men and women. The modern world dates not from the Renaissance, but from the eighteenth century. During this century the male became gradually predominantly rational and utilitarian in dress, while women grew increasingly irrational and frivolous. This justifies my contention that our conception of the world must deeply influence our appearance, while the appearance of our contemporaries modifies our conception of the world.

The Rococo style is the outcome of a *vertical* swing of taste from formality back to informality; from the rational to the intuitive; from the constructed to the organic. It is also the outcome of a *horizontal* movement towards democratic equality, and away from aristocratic privilege and exclusiveness. Although in its refinement and delicacy the aristocratic heritage is clear, there is a good deal more than a hint of the influence of the flourishing upper middle class, for whom money counted quite as much as birth. When the members of the court and the government of France settled into the small *hôtels* and cosy apartments of Paris, thankful to be away from all the draughty, uncomfortable acres of marble and gilded bronze at Versailles, distinctions between the two groups grew hazy – visually at least. For the moment majesty had had its day. The emphasis on comfort was certainly middle class, rather than aristocratic. Rooms began to be filled with furniture of quite a new conception in which the easy accommodation of the body was considered as much as visual effect. Chairs made low to the ground, deep and broad in the seat, with well upholstered backs set at an inclined angle, invited the sitter to lounge diagonally from one side of the widely spreading arms to the other. For happy intimate gatherings of intelligent friends a group of such comfortable chairs would be drawn about the fire, screened from the main area of the room. Gaiety, vivacity, elegance and grace had come to seem more necessary than pomp and circumstance. Ideas were scaled down; the intention was no longer so much to impress as to charm and please. In the decoration of a room the cold formality of marble panels was replaced by the friendly warmth of wood. Left with its natural grain showing, the wood was carved in delicate serpentine lines ('the line of beauty') from which naturalistic leaves and tendrils broke out asymmetrically, to invade the panel or curl over on to its frame. Pretty trophies of pipes and tabors, carved, or painted in pastel colours and only lightly touched with gold, replaced the former glories of shields and helmets, trumpets and drums in solid gilded bronze. Gardening tools, rakes and watering pots, twined with flowers and suspended from ribbon bows, suggested the informality of a pastoral idyll, in which the leisurely courtier, having dismissed his servants, could play music to his equals, or himself make hay – not as a way of life, but as a pleasurable pastime. Necessity was unknown in this world in which the refuge from a constant ceremonial parade was found in the personal performance of plebeian tasks. Mars and Minerva had given way to Daphnis and Chlöe. Comparison of the garden designs on pp. 29, 32 will show how in the latest schemes, wayward and playfully serpentine paths led the promenader a pretty dance, flirting coquettishly now in this corner and now in that, but always with grace and consideration. It is a simple game played at an elevated level, never entirely out of hand, where uncertainty is never menacing. The surprises titillate but do not shock. The gardens of the early eighteenth century are as entirely artificial as those of the seventeenth, but whereas the latter were a setting for a king and his court, the former were intended for a group of elegant friends and playful lovers. Both groups *behaved* themselves: the one, to demand and give respect, the other, to invite and offer affection.

In general terms the Rococo was a reaction in France to the rigid court style designated Classical Baroque. It was nevertheless also a direct development from High Roman Baroque, and continued certain features of that style in modified form. Movement and light are essential to both. The major employment of curving lines and rounded forms is a dominant feature in each, but while Baroque, in either its Roman or Classical manifestations, is always characteristically spacious, gracious, demanding and heroic, the Rococo in any of its varied national interpretations is intimate, graceful, insinuating and domestic. Sometimes, when the style is employed for a public expression, as in the splendid churches of southern Germany, in Juvara's Stupinigi Palace at Turin, or in the frescoes of Giovanni Battista Tiepolo, a clear distinction of category is almost impossible to make. The southern preoccupation with form rather than line, and with reality rather than fantasy, holds always closer to the full-blooded weight and splendour of the High Baroque. Yet even in such exceptions there is a relative gaiety, playfulness and delicacy of colouring, and a conscious elegance which differentiates these works from the more vigorous original expression. The differences and dependencies of the two concepts will be most clearly grasped through a comparison of almost any painting by Rubens with any by Watteau. In the personal style of each artist the style of an age will be found exemplified. The work of Rubens is active, filled with pulsating life and visual drama. His figures, essentially human, are solid and weighty, built upon the grand scale. They are not so much larger than life, as life at its largest. His colours are rich, warm and ceremonial: scarlet, crimson, amber, and deep sapphire blue. His monumental forms are caught in the glowing golden light of a fecund autumn afternoon, suffused with hot dusky brown shadows. There is a sense of ripe harvest splendour, and a sense too of stately ceremony.

A tentative movement towards relaxation in dress appeared as early as the 1670s. (*Femme de qualité en grisette* by St Jean, 1683.)

In contrast, Watteau shows us vulnerably human figures, of a much slighter build, hesitant and timidly confidential. He uses soft and powdery, or delicately opalescent tints rather than full notes of solid colour. He views his scenes through a cool spring haze, by the first washy light of dawn or the pale uncertainty of silvery evening twilight. The full-scale events of Rubens have become for Watteau intimate, fleeting moments. Yet we know that Watteau was a great admirer of Rubens and that he made careful studies from the huge and flamboyant series of allegorical pictures of the *Life of Marie de Medici*. From the power of the Baroque was developed the charm of the Rococo: out of the lion came forth sweetness.

As the natural tendency of the age was towards elegance, elongation and filigreed refinement, attention turned inevitably back beyond the Baroque to Mannerism. Influences from the late sixteenth century upon the eighteenth were many and conscious, as can be seen clearly in the decorative designs of Jean Bérain, for example. Fantasy and exoticism were rife. Furniture was made to appear organic, as if one part grew out of another, while everything was done to disguise its actual construction and decoration flowed unbroken over joints. A *commode* was conceived as a piece of sculpture rather than as a chest-of-drawers. Its *bombée* surface, overlaid with oriental lacquer (chosen for the native use of asymmetrical design), was built carefully to hide all division of the drawers. The lacquer panels were additionally overlaid by naturalistic trails of occidental foliage in fastidiously carved gilded bronze, from which a leaf or tendril curled dimensionally forward to form an unnoticeable handle. But in spite of this fantastic ambiguity, the extreme imaginative paradox of the *threateningly* grotesque was absent. The Baroque renewal of contact between art and nature was never totally denied. Works in the Rococo style have no hardness and no real uncertainty as to gender or intention. The frequent lack of predictability is wayward rather than purposely disturbing. There is always a soft seductiveness, a gentle consideration, an open possibility, and above all, grace, charm and amusement. These were the interests of the age, and they are also to be found in its clothing.

A certain movement towards relaxation appeared, tentatively, in dress as early as the 1670s – first most notably in dress for women. The exact derivation of the sac, mantua or nightgown, has I believe never been quite certainly established. It seems most probable however that it was oriental in origin. Whether Near Eastern or Far Eastern, it was in either case a simple T-shaped construction which had been more or less universal for centuries. Visual evidence suggests that the Islamic caftan was the inspiration for the comfortable house-gown worn by Henry VIII in a portrait of 1542.[5] This Eastern uniform, with its characteristic 'frogged' decoration continued to influence the design of domestic robes for men and women, until well on into the early seventeenth century. Hilliard's miniature of Lord Chancellor Hatton shows him wearing such a gown in the 1580s.[6] A portrait of Lady Scudamore proves that women also still wore an almost identical garment in the second decade of the seventeenth century.[7] Significantly the most informal example of a *robe de chambre*, illustrated in plates of fashionable dress by Jean de St Jean in 1694, is decorated on its front edges by a braided ornament suggestive of 'frogging'. The example of the famous 'Persian Vest', introduced by Charles II (though arguments as to its exact nature still rage), provides evidence that interest in Near Eastern dress was general in the 1660s.[8] It seems then more than probable, in view of the direct trading connections with the Orient through the various East India Companies, that simple, loosely fitted exotic robes may actually have been imported for use in the privacy of the home. There is a long history of women wearing an unfitted informal gown on undress occasions. In 1617 for example Lady Anne Clifford '. . . went to church in my rich night-gown and petticoat'.[9] On 2 March 1669 Mrs Pepys 'this day put on first her French gown, called a Sac'. In 1677 Mrs Aphra Behn referred scathingly to 'Your frugal huswifery Miss in the Pit at a Play, in a long scarf and Night-gown'.[10] Randle Holme

5   Henry VIII in a Velvet Surcoat by Holbein, Castle Howard, York.

6   Victoria and Albert Museum, London.

7   Tate Gallery, London.

8   *See Diaries* by Pepys, Samuel, 8–17 October 1666, and Evelyn, John, 18 October 1666.

9   Clifford, Lady Anne, *Diary*, 28 December 1617.

10   Behn, Mrs Aphra, *The Town Fop*, 1677.

(84.)

The strong, simple colouring of the Neo–classical period is seen in this plate. 'Natural' fabrics and 'masculine' shades, terracotta, dark malachite green, hot ochre, or bright lapis blue were favoured. (From *Costume Parisien*, 1799.)

in *The Academy of Amory* (1688) mentions that 'There is a kind of loose Garment without, and Stiffe Bodies under them and was a great fashion for women about the year 1676. Some called them Mantuas'. As so often in the history of dress, naming is wayward and puzzling, providing a field wide open for scholastic battles; but I would suggest that all such garments were of similar derivation and cut. Also, as so often in the history of fashion, we find writers greeting as a complete innovation a type of dress which has clearly been in constant daily wear for years. Suddenly fashion has need of a change in expression, and taking up the informal for smart wear, gives it a new name and adapts it slightly to a different purpose. It would seem that the important innovation of the 1670s was not the invention, but the adoption, of an informal house-robe as the basis for a new public appearance. The mantua (a corruption of the French *manteau*) is another example of fashion's need to combine different ideas in one composition. The Baroque expression of a loosely fluid, easy-fitting garment has been submitted to the formal restraint of French Classical Baroque by pleating in all fullness, to lie more or less smoothly over rigidly whaleboned stays. In the darkest room on the ground floor of Rosenborg Castle in Copenhagen, there is a wax-work effigy of Queen Sophie-Marie, dating from about 1671, wearing a gown laid in pleats around the *décolleté* neck, which are held in again by a band at the waist. No doubt each pleat is in fact caught-down beneath the fold to mould the upper part into the shape of the defining whalebone body. Such a gown provided the most *avant-garde* fashion for the closing decades of the seventeenth century. In spite of the rigid etiquette at Versailles – or more probably because of it – fashionable people tried to run the gauntlet by striking a compromise between formality and informality. Similar compromises are found in all the decorative designs for furniture, tapestry and embroidery made by the court artist Jean Bérain at this time. A great stickler for established rules, like the Duchess of Orléans, boasted that she never wore anything but *grand habit* (the boned bodice and trained skirt discussed in the last chapter), or riding dress. She wrote: 'I have never worn a *robe-de-chambre* nor a mantua and have only one *robe-de-nuit* for getting-up in the morning and going to bed at night.' Clearly she disapproved of what was creeping into general practice during the 1690s. By that time, even in quite formal dress, the bodice and train were often replaced by the gown or mantua, given an appearance of formality by the neatness of the pleating of the body part. Informality of detail was added, like the 'Steinkirk' cravat, borrowed from the male wardrobe, and the lavish fall of layered lace flounces at the elbow. During this decade, too, fashionable trimming on the petticoat (except for the most formal occasions) tended away from the massed splendours of thick metallic embroidery, bullion fringe and tassels, towards loosely gathered flounces of lace or self-fabric. In conjunction with the fully pleated sleeves, the open skirt of the mantua, piled-up behind into a billowing, blousy bustle, increased the effect of casualness with which women moved into the new century.

The importance of the mantua is not confined to the fact that it introduced the first intimation of ideas which were to be developed later as a true Rococo expression of relaxed informality. It was also the first outer-

A general air of nonchalance was carefully cultivated by the decade of the 1690s. (*Homme de qualité en habit garny d'agrémens* by St Jean, 1693.)

garment (as opposed to underwear) to be made by women for women. From about 1675, as the making of female clothing began to pass from the province of the tailor to that of the dressmaker, femininity became for the first time a very conscious attribute of dress. A new declaration that it was more seemly for women's clothes to be the product of female workers indicates a marked change of attitude. Except for formal court wear, women's dress would increasingly emphasize softness, prettiness and delicacy. The earliest mantuas were of extremely simple construction. Two lengths of fabric were laid in pleats over the shoulder, to fall to the ground at front and back, being then seamed together centrally behind and under each arm. The fullness was drawn into pleats to define the body, and released at the waist to allow fullness in the skirt. The sleeves were straight strips of pleated fabric set horizontally into the almost unshaped armhole.[11] Only very slight refinements of this system provided the basis for dress during the major part of the eighteenth century.

During the 1670s, male clothing, through its uniform appearance, was already moving towards that expression of equality which was to become important later. Here too there were indications of a relaxation of constraint by the 1690s. Although the body of the coat was still cut closely, extra fullness began to be added at each side of the skirt. The sleeves ceased to fit closely to the arm, being gently widened from shoulder to wrist, and there turned back into opulent cuffs. The really *avant-garde* would appear often without a waistcoat, but with the shirt blousing out and the cravat informally and loosely knotted, its ends tucked up to one side into one of the buttonholes of the coat. The side lappets of the wig were thrown back off the shoulder, and a general air of nonchalance was most carefully affected.

> Did you mark the Beau tiff off his wig, what a deal of pains he took to toss it back, when the very weight thereof was like to draw him from his seat?[12]

> There is a fat fellow whom I have long remarked, wearing his breast open in the midst of winter. . . . A sincere heart has not made half so many conquests as an open waistcoat.[13]

This appears perhaps a mere revival of the unfastened slovenliness which had expressed the fluidity and plasticity of High Baroque, but the intervening period of formality and polished manners had left its mark. The new negligence was of a lighter, slighter, more graceful kind than the full-blooded panache of the 1630s. It pointed forward rather than back.

The ease and informality, which had been gradually gaining strength in all areas, became very marked by the turn of the century. It is almost fully realized by Bernard Picart in his sketch for a *fête galante* made in 1708. Here the gathered flounces on the woman's petticoat; the width of the pleated sleeves and the size of her deep cuffs; the copious and rounded form of her fontange (so different in effect from the sharp, neat narrowness of the towering caps of the 1690s), all proclaim a changing spirit. The loose 'pagoda' shape of the man's sleeve, the fullness of his coat skirts and his casually arranged wig, together with the very unconventional pose of the figures, speak of that release which had been given a slight official sanction by the king in 1699.

By the 1720s, as the Rococo spirit moved towards a climax, clothes acquired an even more easy grace. During the Régence Paris saw the complete adoption of a négligé appearance. The costume of the boudoir had descended to the drawing-room. The 'private' quality of dress was emphasized by the general use of forms distinctly 'undress' in origin. The fullness of the mantua was at last allowed to hang free from the shoulders, all definition of the figure lost within its swaying folds. The sacque, the *robe battante*, the *robe volante* – the robes which swing and float – have all the appearance of complete freedom, whatever confining stays might be worn beneath. After about 1710 the wide skirts of the loose gown were

11 *See* Arnold, Janet, *A Mantua at Clive House Museum* (Costume Society Bulletin No. 4, 1970).

12 *Spectator.*

13 'The Levellers, a Dialogue between two young Ladies concerning Matrimony' in *The Harleian Miscellany*, 1744–6.

supported again on hoops of cane or whalebone, to impart an extra air of lightness to the crisp thin silks, as though the dress was inflated and really floated like a balloon. The constant heaving and billowing of these airy silken sacks must have given an appearance at once light, frivolous, excited, sensuous and feminine. The colours most in favour were fresh and clear and 'feminine' – tints of rose, shell-pink, pale apple or jade green, daffodil or saffron yellow; or delicately muted – dove-colour, soft lilac, powder-blue; all spiced with the occasional deeper more 'masculine' note of sea-water green, chestnut brown or a full scarlet. Heads were simpler now, dressed in small neat spheres of bubbling curls, covered by the merest wisp of lace or lawn.

As hoops distended women's gowns, the skirts of men's coats too grew much more full. Circles of fabric were set into fan-pleats on each hip, held out by interlinings of horse-hair cloth, and edged with wire, to give a light and lively balletic spring, more volatile than the heavy weight of the 1690s smart coat.

The skirts of your fashionable coats form as large a circumference as our petticoats; as these are set out with whalebone so are those with wire, to encrease and sustain the bunch of folds that hang down at each side.[14]

The new ease and informality was fully realized by Bernard Picart in his sketch for a *fête galante*. (*The Music Lesson*, 1708.)

14 *Spectator*, No. 145, 1711.

The male wig was also simpler. Its front and side wings were cut short, and dressed in horizontal curls, the long back tresses tied by a velvet ribbon at the nape, or hidden in a black silk bag.

Onwards into the 1730s there was always the air of an impromptu party indoors or out, luxurious, extravagant, highly finished, but without ceremony. The women were loosely draped in yielding, easily disarranged, partly concealing, partly revealing robes. The men were spruce and smart, in cleanly fitted garments with a sprightly dash. Everything proclaims an artfully sophisticated attitude of mind in which nothing is to be taken too seriously, and everything is to be treated as a sensuous game, to which the new conception of costume could add an even more sophisticated spice.

> Prithee Cloe, not so fast,
> Let's not run and Wed in haste
> We've a thousand things to do,
> You must flye, and I persue;
> You must frown, and I must sigh;
> I intreat, and you deny.
> Stay – If I am never crost,
> Half the Pleasure will be lost;
> Be, or seem to be severe,
> Give me reason to Despair;
> Fondness will my Wishes cloy,
> Make me careless of the Joy.
> Lovers may of course complain
> Of their trouble and their pain;
> But if pain and Trouble cease,
> Love without it will not please.[15]

Men now constantly pay court, in art, and clearly women are in the ascendant. As in the middle of the nineteenth century, when feminine power increased to dominate completely in the domestic field, so here, women visibly occupy a larger space, with confidence.

Distinctions between the dress of the two sexes became even more clearly marked, though textiles themselves were not yet allocated completely into two groups, each for application to only one sex. Silk, embroidery and lace, still interchangeable, were less so than formerly. The lighter weights of taffeta and satin were used for women's clothes; heavier silk and velvet for men's. Thick encrustations of gold thread and spangles were still employed to decorate masculine dresswear, but its limits were now firmly proscribed to trimming down the fronts, round the pocket-holes and on the cuffs. These limits were to be, year by year, more narrowly controlled. In the uniform of coat, waistcoat and breeches, the tendency was to confine obvious display to the only partially visible waistcoat. Lace, much softer, lighter and prettier than any seventeenth-century types, while it was used in increasingly deep and layered furbelows or *engageantes* to cascade about a woman's elbows, appeared only as a narrow frill at a man's wrist and shirt front. Shoes were now totally different. Those for women, high-heeled and needle-pointed at the toe, produced an optical illusion of minute delicacy. Those for men,

In the 1720s, the Rococo spirit moved towards its climax with clothes displaying an extreme, easy grace. Notice the obvious differentiation between the shoes of the two sexes by this date. The woman's dress is the so-called *robe volante*. (*The Alarm* by Jean François de Troy, 1723.)

Overleaf
During the 1770s, one of the very few innovations of the period appeared: the *polonaise*. On p. 114 the woman to the left wears her skirt trussed into the pocket hole – a familiar gesture. On p. 115 compare the children's clothing with that of the small boy illustrated on p. 54. (*Left: The Kiss* from *La Nouvelle Héloïse* by J. M. Moreau *le jeune. Right: Le Rendez-vous pour Marly* by Moreau, 1776.)

15 Oldmixen, John (1673–1742).

Undress clothes became ever
more prominent in public
appearance, while the *grand-habit*
of full court dress was limited to
only the most formal of
occasions, and consisted of
various survivals from past
fashion. The whalebone body
and trained overskirt dates from
the seventeenth century, the
wide oval hoop from the mid-
eighteenth, and only the
trimming of the petticoat is
up to date in the neo-Classical
manner. (*La dame du palais de la
reine* by Moreau, 1777.)

low-heeled, rationally shaped, neatly buckled, seem deliberately understated.

During the first half of the century, patterned fabrics, such as brocade
or damasks, in large and bold designs, formed an important subject for
seasonal change at a time when interest in cut and form was distinctly
limited. The highest accomplishment a dressmaker could show was in
the skill with which she arranged the pattern to balance perfectly in the
various sections of the robe. In general, as interest in textile design began
to fade towards the middle of the century, patterns grew first smaller and
more haphazardly asymmetrical; and by the 1770s tended to be limited to
tiny sprigs scattered between narrow stripes. From the 1750s a newer
interest appeared which lent itself even more appropriately to a dis-
tinctively feminine effect. This was the work of the *modiste*. While the
construction of dress continued hardly changed, the decoration of its
surface grew increasingly elaborate. Exuberant *échelles* of puffy ribbon
bows bubbled down the front of a stomacher. Garlands of artificial
flowers bobbed on the wavy rivulets of closely ruffled bands of silk, which
curled and meandered on the edges of the gown, and round the petticoat.
Layered swags and flounces, each edged with nodding fringe, and interspersed with tassels, ropes of beads, ribbon loops and valances of lace,
foamed and rustled about the fashionable figure. All bear witness to a new
passion for novelty of an ephemeral nature. Easily crushed and spoiled,
they added to the effect of a pretty, fragile but futile femininity. While
dressmakers plodded on, only gradually perfecting their craft, it was the
modiste who reaped the full fruit of victory, allowing her invention and
ingenuity free rein in a new art – the improvisation of surface ornament
for the basic dress, and the creation of another new frivolity, feminine
millinery. The one area of dress in which is found an effect of grotesque
monstrosity comparable, though not identical to that which had been
used by Mannerism, was the dressing of the hair. Augmented by pounds
of false plaits and tresses, piled over pads, caked with pomatum, filled with
pins and covered with powder, the hair was raised to an exaggerated
height. These elaborate arrangements of fantasy were a very late manifestation of the Rococo spirit, not appearing until well into the 1760s after
the main impetus had passed.

One of the very few innovations in the form of eighteenth-century
dress appeared even later, during the 1770s: the *polonaise*. Like so many
fashions, its beginning may be found in the way in which existing clothes
were adapted to daily wear. For many years it had been usual while
engaged in any active pursuit, to 'truss the gown in the pocket holes'.[16]
The majority of dresses had an opening in the seam on each hip, allowing
access to the separate bag-pockets which were tied around the waist on a
tape below the petticoat. As the petticoat was fashionably instep length,
while the gown was invariably trained, a busy woman would take the
two bottom front corners of the open robe, turn them inwards and pull
them through the pocket-holes. The skirt of the robe was thus drawn up
into a bouffant swag behind. The *polonaise*, and its many variants, like the
circassienne, were formalizations of this practice, in which the skirt of an
open-fronted dress was gathered into three large festoons. A late manifestation of the Rococo spirit (or, in its formalization of an informal

16   *See* Willet-Cunnington, C.,
*Handbook of English Costume in
the 18th Century* (London, 1957).

Informality of dress in England was not that of the boudoir, as in France, but the casual utility of country wear, epitomized in Gainsborough's painting. The man wears a 'frock', the woman a sack-backed, hip-length jacket and matching petticoat. Such jackets were variously named *casquin*, *caraco* or *pet-en-l'air*. (*Mr and Mrs Andrews* by Thomas Gainsborough, *c.* 1750.)

manner, a precursor of Neo-classicism) it added possibility to the expression of a light and buoyant feminine casualness. Such 'undress' clothes formed an ever more prominent part in public appearance, while the *grand-habit* of full court-dress was limited only to the most formal of occasions.

So far my consideration has been confined to France, since it was to Paris that all Europe still turned for leadership in fashionable matters. There society grouped around a hostess. The *salon* was the centre for intellectual, artistic and political discussion. In England things were different. Here there had been no powerful monarch to concentrate and centralize a court. The English temperament had always been characterized by informality, independence and a dislike of fussy affectation. The aristocracy preferred to be away from the centre, living in the splendour of their new country houses, rather than shuffling between urban lodgings and an old-fashioned ramshackle Tudor palace. In 1715, England did not experience the sense of relief that was felt in France. There had been no iron grip to exercise a control too firm. While the full excesses of the Roman Baroque had been tamed in France, they had passed almost unheeded in England, which was too occupied with middle-class revolt to worry over less insistent matters. Now a temperamental preference

A Meissen group, *c.* 1775–80, wearing the popular *caraco* jackets and aprons with large pockets.

for compromise and understatement found its own level in the simple country villa architecture of the Venetian, Andrea Palladio, known principally through the work of Inigo Jones. In 1715 there was an English event to mark the beginning of a more modest manifestation of the Rococo ideal, which at first glance appears almost unconnected with, even contrary to, its continental counterpart. In that year appeared the first volume of *Vitruvius Britannicus*, a work celebrating the ideas of the first-century Roman architect, and all his many later disciples, among whom Palladio and Jones were numbered, as well as the young designer Colen Campbell and his patron Lord Burlington. In a rather different way from fashionable France, England, too, looked back at just the same time, towards her own modest variants of High Baroque and Mannerism. By doing so, a characteristic appearance was created for the eighteenth century; the classically inspired country villa, set in an artificially contrived imitation of the 'natural' Italian *campagna*. This was the great English contribution to the Rococo style. When not on their country estates, the aristocracy found a social centre in town at the coffee-house and the club, both exclusively masculine preserves. A totally differently orientated society from that of France was not unaffected by the spirit of its age, though naturally the resulting expression was unique. A manifestation of Rococo style as fully characteristic as anything from France is found in the work of Hogarth and Gainsborough. The difference is that of detail and degree. Although the subject-matter is utterly unlike, there is a complete equality in composition, delicacy and sumptuous sensuality of technique. These artists depict a less artificial, less well mannered, more naturalistic and much darker world, than the dream-like ideal created by the French. But here nevertheless is informality, charm, vivacity, a bubbling gaiety, creamy paint, feathery application and a delight in the s-shaped, scrolling 'line of beauty' which will be found to control all the composition.

In dress, the informality of England was not the informality of the boudoir. It was the casual utility of country wear. In the loose frock-coat designed for shooting, a man could stand relaxed. To women the trailing mantua seemed less suitable than the subdued simplicity of the *caraco*. This short, jacket-like bodice, spreading into a hip-length basque, and worn only with a short petticoat and apron, had formed the daily wear of peasant women for generations. There is an English angularity to be noted in the shape of the side-hoop which, fashionably, gave some slight *élan* to an understated theme. Its squareness only palely reflects the more elegantly buoyant and vivacious variations from across the Channel. Plainer fabrics, and simple, straw, milk-maid hats give a slight touch of Arcadian delights, which is more realistic and less theatrical than any French version of the same theme. But it was this characteristic, unaffected statement made in England which attracted the attention of the French before the century was over. Like called to like. English gardens began to appear in France. French women wearing caracos of painted chintz or printed calico and spreading aprons with large useful pockets wandered in their winding walks. French men ordered English carriages and horses, and a very few appeared rather artificially *en jockie*. The full Rococo impetus had passed, however, long before. The main background, against which such romantically Anglophile French importations were seen, was Neo-classical. In 1762 Madame Pompadour, so ardently Rococo in her dressing, commissioned the chaste rectangularity of the Petit Trianon. When Thomas Chippendale published *The Gentleman and Cabinet-Makers Director* (1754), filled with scrolling 'French' designs, its influence, though wide, was even then principally popular and provincial. All over Europe the really fashionable had already sensed another spirit in the air. Herculaneum and Pompeii were being excavated in the 1740s. In 1755, Winckelmann's *Reflections on the Imitation of Greek Works of Art in Painting and Sculpture* appeared in Germany, and Piranesi produced his powerful engravings, *Le Antichita Romane*, in 1756. Frivolity and informality no longer satisfied. Intellectual theories and a high seriousness marked a newer mood.

Neo-classical designs. (From
Household Furniture by Thomas
Hope, 1807.)

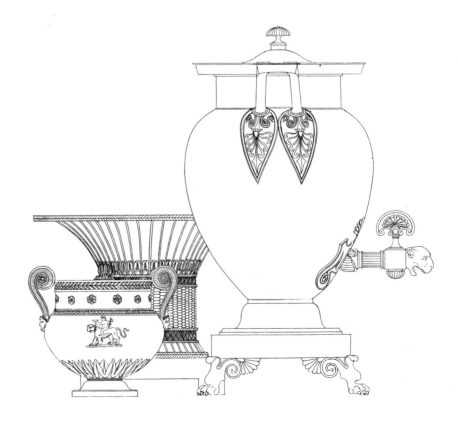

Neo-classicism

Liberty had always held her seat in this country . . . before the increasing light of reason had shown to its inhabitants the blessings of entire freedom.

This body, marked by no vein, moved by no nerve, is animated by a celestial spirit which courses like a sweet vapour through every part.

Johann Joachim Winckelmann

It is not only in charming the eyes that great works of art have attained their aim, it is in penetrating the soul, it is in making on the spirit a profound impression akin to reality.

Jacques-Louis David

A belated example of English Rococo is to be found in the 'Gothick' revival of the mid-eighteenth century. When seen at its most characteristic, as in the decoration of Horace Walpole's villa, 'Strawberry Hill', or in the Gothick Chamber at Claydon House in Buckinghamshire, the reasons for including such work in this particular category will be self-evident. No serious attempt *appears* to have been made to recapture the essential spirit of the late Gothic world. Architectural motifs have been borrowed for purely decorative purposes. Made spindly, delicate and amusing they have been playfully applied, simply as ornament, like the icing on a cake. And yet, what at first sight may well seem mere frivolity, should not too much deceive. This was the second Gothic revival to take place in England, and like its predecessor of the late sixteenth century, this newer variation on the theme was at heart equally romantically motivated. Walpole's novel, *The Castle of Otranto* (1764), gives us the clue. Yet the author plainly saw Gothick as an opposing force against the licence and imbecility of 'Chinoiserie', and all the other scrolling asymmetry of the Rococo style. He insisted upon correct archaeological sources. Speaking in later life of his earlier attempts at Gothick decoration he was to say, 'every true Goth must perceive that they [the rooms at Strawberry Hill] are more the works of fancy than imitation'. He saw that they fell short of his ideal. Careful consideration of every aspect of English creations in the Rococo style must draw attention to the fact than an inherent romanticism, with its accompanying interest in the direct appeal of nature, is inextricably woven into the more dominant themes of the age. Indeed, it often seems to meet them sympathetically. It was this essentially romantic spirit, rather than an already *passé* interest in Rococo itself, which attracted French attention. In France expression of this interest reached a climax at the end of the century in the austere abstract geometry, the awe-inspiring severity of Boullée's monumental projects; and the uncompromising architecture of Ledoux – 'neither utilitarian nor merely ornamental, neither anti-classical nor revivalist'[1] – but certainly romantic in spirit and effect.

Examination of the two works already cited at the end of the last chapter, those of Piranesi and Winckelmann, show that when the former viewed all the splendour and immensity of Roman ruins, he was so awestruck and emotionally stirred, that his illustrations were suffused, perhaps unconsciously, with romantic overtones, while the latter wrote equally romantically, from a poetic sensitivity, which could see only the sublime purity of Greek antiquities. These antagonistic individuals were key figures who helped to crystallize the concept, emerging in the 1760s, which we know as Neo-classicism.

Contemporary with Walpole's typically English, amateur folly at Strawberry is another folly which was built in the park of Hagley Hall in Worcestershire in 1758. Designed by James 'Athenian' Stuart, it is in the form of a small Greek temple of 'an early, an inelegant and unenriched Doric, that affords no details',[2] a style then considered 'ruder than Gothick' and entirely uncouth. For its date, it is remarkably heavy and stark; and it was clearly an attempt to evoke the atmosphere of an unsophisticated and 'natural' antiquity, without compromise. Not for another thirty years or more would the Doric order be seen in general 'as the product of an uncorrupted people living close to nature, and thus the purest expression of an architectural ideal – the equivalent of Homeric poetry and Greek vase painting. Primitive, masculine, unencumbered by superfluous ornament, and of a crystalline integrity'.[3] Yet, for a playful age, the Doric temple at Hagley had provided an amusing fantasy.

With these few facts we see the problems which must be faced when trying to formulate a definition of the stylistic expression of the later eighteenth century. Neo-classicism is claimed as the puritan reaction against both the theatrical emotionalism of the Baroque, and the sensuous seductiveness of the Rococo. It is seen as the blow struck against all the 'superfluous ornament' and the 'parading of difficulties at the expense of clearness' which, the composer Gluck asserted, had reduced opera, 'the most splendid and most beautiful of spectacles, into the most ridiculous and wearisome'. Yet Gluck's own attempt at natural sincerity in his opera

1 Honour, Hugh, *Neo-classicism* (London, 1968).

2 Adam, James, *On the Temple at Paestum*, 1761.

3 Honour, Hugh, op. cit.

Orpheo ed Euridice (1762), notably continued the absurdly unnatural convention of employing a castrato voice for the male lead. Clearly, whatever its protagonists believed, Neo-classicism is 'really only a part of a much wider process, the Romantic Movement'.[4] It is surely true that although superficially it may seem 'to be a case of two rival movements – Neo-classicism standing for order, logic, restraint and even a certain puritanism; while Romanticism stood . . . for the free expression of individual passions, regardless of the consequences, and equally regardless of conventional notions of morality. Yet at a deeper level, the rivals are linked; Neo-classicism is one of the many manifestations of the Romantic spirit, with its high ideals, its nostalgia for the past, and its hopes for the future'.[5] Ideas, in fact, which might be summarized as comprising liberty, equality and antiquity.

Despite the deceptive and only relative freedom of the styles of dressing which I have claimed as Baroque and Rococo, fashionable European clothing, for both sexes, in general had been physically restrictive in a high degree for over four hundred years. Complaints against it were exceptional, and quite unheeded, but when Jean-Jacques Rousseau published his novel, *Emile*, in 1762, a more sympathetic climate apparently existed – surely partly created by the effectiveness of the Rococo spirit of freedom in expression. This time the complaint was based not on Christian or on moral grounds, but on rational and hygienic principles.

> The French style of dress uncomfortable and unhealthy for a
> man, is especially bad for children. The stagnant humours, whose
> circulation is interrupted, putrify in a state of inaction and this
> process proceeds more rapidly in an inactive and sedentary life;
> they become corrupt and give rise to scurvy; this disease which is
> continually on the increase among us, was almost unknown to the
> ancients whose way of dressing and living protected them from it.

Fashionable dressing can never, of course, take the slightest account of either aesthetic, moral or hygienic principles, if these happen to be contrary to its vital expression of the moment. When Rousseau's book was published, its success was partly due to the fact that ideas were already swinging towards a less abstracted view of the human body than anything acceptable for centuries. As early as 1752 an English writer had complained of the continuing restriction of formal French dress, noting:

> I frequently sighed for my little loose Frock which I look upon as
> an Emblem of our happy Constitution, for it lays a Man under no
> uneasy Restraint, but leaves it in his Power to do as he pleases.[6]

Meanwhile, fashionable women began to be represented by fashionable painters, wearing classically inspired studio draperies, instead of smart formal wear. In one of his *Discourses*[7] Sir Joshua Reynolds rationally explains that such visual reference, by assuring a mental association with the finest works of the past, would suggest to the viewer that the painting was possessed of greater excellences than it might otherwise be allowed. Although twenty years or more were to pass before such garments

4 Pevsner, Nikolaus, *An Outline of European Architecture* (London, 1943).

5 Lucie-Smith, Edward, *Eroticism in Western Art* (London, 1972).

6 Murphy, Arthur, *Gray's-Inn Journal*, 1752.

7 Reynolds, Joshua, *Discourses*, No. 7, 10 December 1776.

became anything but a studio fantasy, fashionable faces were appearing above bodies seemingly naturally shaped by the artist, and the idea of liberty was making a tentative public appearance. It was probably smiled upon simply as a visual change rather than as a physical relief. When, by the late 1790s, a much adapted but certainly classically inspired dress had become a fact, not a fiction, Sir William Wraxall, looking back on it from 1815, saw it as:

> finally levelling or obliterating almost all external distinction of costume between the highest and the lowest of the sex in the country.[8]

Perhaps the first clear notes of liberty and equality had been struck in children's dress. Rousseau had advised, against all current practice:

> When the child draws its first breath do not confine it in tight wrappings. No cap, no bandages, nor swaddling clothes. Loose and flowing flannel wrappers which leave its limbs free and are not too heavy to check his movements, not too warm to prevent his feeling air . . . the limbs of a growing child should be free to move easily in his clothing; nothing should cramp their growth or movement; there should be nothing tight, nothing fitting closely to the body, no belts of any kind. . . . The best plan is to keep children in frocks as long as possible and then to provide them with loose clothing, without trying to define the shape which is only another way of deforming it. Their defects of body and mind may all be traced to the same source, the desire to make men of them before their time.[9]

Here was anticipation indeed! Until this time the smallest child had been dressed exactly as a miniature adult. By the 1780s, liberating garments had not only become the general rule for children, but mothers too were adopting a simple frock for the morning at least. As yet, small boys in their loose trousers *en Matelot* were in advance of their fathers by ten years. An undeniable prompting towards a new appearance for adults is found in the radical reformation of children's clothing. The mind was being encouraged to question all the rules, as fashionably enlightened mothers began to breast-feed their own children, often openly, surrounded by admiring friends. The established social order, and Christianity itself were being criticized as never before. The pages of the new *Encyclopedia* (the first volume of which had appeared in 1751) encouraged the claims of experience and reason over those of revelation.

Yet other enlightened ideas, first formulated in the intimate conversation of informal Rococo *salons*, had actively erupted in the 1770s through the American War of Independence, and culminated in the Revolution in France during the nineties. Concurrently a new liberty and equality was manifest in dress. There the liberty and equality did not in fact result from the political upheavals, or even reflect them, but formed an alternative expression of identical forces. As with Enlightened political thinking, the betrayer of the old order sprang from within and did not attack from without.

8 Wraxall, Sir Nathaniel William, *Historical and Posthumous Memoirs*, 1815.

see also
Glenbervie, Lord, *Journals*, 1794, quoted in Waugh, N., *The Cut of Men's Clothes* (London, 1964):

'I have also heard Fox say that the neglect of dress in people of fashion had, he thought, contributed much to propagate levelling and equalising notions.'

9 Rousseau, translated by B. Foxley, *Emile* (London, 1911) and reprinted from Everyman's Library edition by permission of J. M. Dent & Sons Ltd.

Politically, and aesthetically too (as at the Renaissance) inspiration was found once again in the definitive statements of the Classical World. But for the first time in the history of Europe – or for the first time quite so completely and consistently – fashionable women found inspiration for the *form* of their dress in styles from the past. Any earlier influences had been limited to details, decorations, or to a fanciful manner of wearing contemporary dress. While women were about to embark upon a series of romantic imitations, beginning with the antique, men, looking forward to a functional future, pared away the splendours which had so long provided the signs of rank and power, and concentrated instead on the antique spirit of democracy. They found that spirit already suitably expressed in the levelling equality of country clothing, rather than in the original garments of antiquity. By 1785, the new ideas had been sufficiently assimilated into fashionable dress to be easily discernible – perhaps most easily at that date in England. Two major political revolutions had already occurred here in the seventeenth century tending to the establishment of democratic principles. Current agrarian and industrial experiments were still further changing the social structure. Since the execution of Charles I the Court had hardly counted as a focus for fashion, and English tradition had always shown a marked preference for the privacy of country and domestic life, as opposed to continental urban and public formality.

Feminine fashions of the 1780s were based upon the close-bodied gown, of a type which had been favoured in England throughout the century. Directly descended from the mantua of the late seventeenth century, it retained the definition of the torso, and now had long, closely fitted sleeves. The full skirt was only moderately distended over a hip-pad, or 'false-rump' sometimes made from cork. (Even in the 1770s it had become quite usual for the smartest English women to wear formal gowns without hoops or panniers when in the privacy of their own homes.) The low neck of the dress was in general modestly filled by a bouffant gauzy kerchief. A wide ribbon sash encircled the natural waist, to emphasize the trend towards a shorter, less restrictive bodice. Hats were large and assertive. Wide brimmed and deep crowned, they were loaded with ribbon bows and feathers, and were usually worn over a big, generously frilled mob-cap in a final French-inspired flourish of Rococo fantasy. Apart from this feature, the dress was relatively simple and undemanding. Men already displayed the neatness, careful grooming and that undemonstrative look for which George Brummell is so often given the entire credit. Frequently dark in colour, the suit was made from fine wool cloth for all but the most formal of occasions; prevented from passing as unstylish by its close yet unrestricting fit and such details as plate buttons as big as a tenpenny-piece. The formal hat with a three-cornered cock was often, even in town, replaced by a low-crowned, wide-brimmed round hat, an informal shape of sporting origin. This blending together of dressiness and informality gave to the clothing of both men and women at this time a typically English quality of non-commitment to clear alternatives; that tendency to compromise which seems so hypocritical to others. Was it *rus in urbe* or *urbs in rure*? Dressed in such clothes, a young couple might either be strolling in one of the new London squares, or out viewing their country estates.

This picture from the late eighteenth century illustrates the mutual admiration of the French and English in matters of taste and dress. Sir Brooke lies romantically, dressed in the best English casual manner, handling a volume by Rousseau. (*Sir Brooke Boothby* by Joseph Wright of Derby, 1781.)

In France at the same time the smartest form of dress for women was *à l'Anglaise*, that same close-bodied gown which had overtaken in popularity the more typically French style with a pleated sack-back. But in its trimming and attention to detail (the work of the *modiste*), there was evident a fully-committed inventiveness and thoughtful precision – a serious attitude to frivolity. Delicate, but firmly stated, the points would be acutely made. There would be a conscious *chic*, quite unlike the 'throw-away' effects cultivated in England; something to assure, still, the dominant position of Paris as a mecca for the ultra-smart. Masculine clothes, though similar in cut and construction to an English suit, with narrow shoulder, close body, tight sleeves and form-defining breeches, would on all occasions be more distinctly formal. More frequently the coat would be made from silk, in a plain colour, with a minute pattern, or smart narrow stripes; and also would more frequently be decorated very lightly with delicate embroidery.

If the English looked aloof and non-committal to the Continentals, French dress could illustrate in its self-possessed distinction Horace Walpole's assertion of 'the violent vanity of the French'. Fashion at this time was much affected by that eternal love–hate relationship between the two nations. A mixture of admiration and irritation on both sides will allow neither to ignore the other for any length of time. Something of the mutual admiration of the day is nicely blended in Joseph Wright's portrait of Sir Brooke Boothby. He was painted in 1781, lying romantic-ally but well dressed in a woodland glade, rather carelessly handling an original manuscript by Rousseau. Rousseau himself admired much that was English, in particular the writing of the philosopher Locke, while England found in Rousseau's writing a definitive and sympathetic state-ment of much which had always been instinctive to her. So, too, France could find a natural expression of that equality which her political thinking was beginning insistently to demand in the informality of English country dress. In addition to its subject-matter, Wright's picture is visually typical of its era. Neo-classical in the cool clarity and hard-edged precision of its technique, the portrait is Romantic in its conception, content and inten-tion. In this picture there seems an almost conscious reference to late sixteenth-century paintings of well-dressed young men reclining in abstracted melancholy among trees, wearing wide-brimmed hats. Or is this perhaps simply a spontaneous expression of a constant preoccupation with pastoral romance, shared by England with the antique world? Whatever mixed motives prompted the precise details of the picture, the subdued and rather uneventful clothes are worn with a most natural casualness – the sleeves and waistcoat of the pale snuff-brown suit only partly buttoned. Such negligence was soon exaggerated into a far more studied affectation in France.

An example of really advanced French dress for women in 1783 is provided in a famous portrait of Queen Marie Antoinette painted by Vigée-Lebrun. A great sensation was created by the public exhibition of this record of a costume created for the privacy of Trianon. The majority considered it remarkably improper for royalty to be celebrated in a chemise. Her *robe du matin* (accompanied by the simplest straw hat) is of the finest, softest muslin made *à la mode Créole* – an adaptation of the casual provincial dress worn in the planters' society of the French West Indies. Probably not in fact quite as easy as it looks, the Queen's dress would almost certainly have been worn over stays, even if only over a half-boned corset. Nevertheless, visually it is both liberating and egali-tarian. The enemy was indeed within the ranks of the old order when from the inmost circle such a person could declare so openly that she was tired of self-imposed formality and restraint. No wonder the majority was outraged. While hardly classical in form or inspiration, it is clear from this example that only a very few steps more were required to achieve that natural appearance of the body upon which classical styles depended. When Marie Antoinette was thirty, in 1785, she decided that for the future her dresses must be made without the frivolous additions more suitable to younger women; neither would she wear among other things, those liberating, egalitarian garments, the chemise, *Lévites* and robes *à la Turque*, of which only two years before she had been the champion. No individual is entirely consistent, but then individuals do not set fashions. They can only encourage or reinforce what is already happening, when their own inclination and personality coincide opportunely with the general mood of the moment. Now, whatever the Queen of France might say, it was far too late. The *robe du matin* grew steadily more general and less constricting. One example from the *Galérie des Modes* for 1787 is described as *à l'Anglaise*. There seems little to distinguish it from that *à la mode Créole* worn by the Queen herself five years earlier. In 1786 Betsy Sheridan had advised:

> you may tell her as a friend gradually to reduce her Stuffing as
> Rumps are quite out in France and are decreasing here, but can not
> be quite given up till the weather grows warmer.

Any good dressmaker must be aware however that *some* 'stuffing' would still be essential to achieve the stylish effect suggested by this plate. 'Rumps' were by no means universally 'out in France' even in the smart circles which promenaded through the shopping arcades of the Palais Royal. Although still very fully dressed, the coiffure was shrinking in dimension, and the headgear (this one romantically *à la couronne d'amour*) tended to lose the brim as the volume of the dress itself grew less. Clearly, give-and-take between France and England continued in importance. Here France takes English informal casualness, and gives it *chic*, a conscious calculation and high finish, as opposed to instinctive understatement, and displays it very notably upon a figure posed in direct imitation of the antique. Slowly liberty, equality and antiquity drew together, towards the century's close. At the same time, young men in France interpreted the dress of the English country gentleman with great panache and in rather more *voyant* silks and stripes than any to be seen at home. All that Englishmen did instinctively, however romantically or functionally, the Frenchmen did, both romantically and ornamentally, but with calculation.

Although the Bastille fell in 1789, life must have drifted on with little immediate change for many, even at the heart of the trouble. However completely cataclysmic any crisis may seem with hindsight, it is a gradual development, and while actually in process the full catastrophe is not nearly so noticeable. Only after it is over do its effects become entirely apparent. Meanwhile fashion continues its own slow evolution, almost unaffected by outside influences, since it is itself an aspect of those influences. Right up until the execution of Louis XVI in 1793, smart society continued to gather together, and dress continued slowly to move towards an irrevocable transformation. In pictures painted by the fashion-conscious Boilly and Mallet, during the very years of extreme crisis, an earlier tradition of sharply defined, stiffly sumptuous silk is shown blending together with the emerging style of softly fluid, light-weight prettiness; and the massive abstractions of millinery are seen to be evolving into a newer more delicate modesty. Adaptations were gradual. Even the violently revolutionary, but sartorially conventional Robespierre was recorded

Galérie des modes et costumes français, 1787, describes this dress as *Robe du matin à l'Anglaise*, although it seems little different from that *à la mode Créole* worn by Queen Marie-Antoinette five years earlier.

by Boilly, wearing a coat of pale powder-blue striped silk, with a velvet collar.

Meanwhile portraits painted in America for a mixed society based upon a tradition of independent *émigré* revolt against oppressively established orders, show that far away from the main social centres and the traditional trend-setters, the modest adaptations of the middle classes took on an appearance of distinct modishness. As the fashionable ideal of the polite world scaled down its effects towards something more domestic and less theatrical, two traditions, the aristocratic and the bourgeois met almost for the first time on common ground. The middle classes no longer needed to race after their superiors; those superiors seemed to be running towards them with outstretched arms of welcome. Even in 1794, the year of the 'Terror' in France (the year when to be seen in anything but the simplest kind of clothes could probably mean arrest), it would seem from visual evidence that fashionable dress all over Europe had become so modest that few really smart people could have been thought provocative by any 'people's government'. The most understated of short-waisted 'little-girl' frocks would surely have passed without comment in Paris itself. As the vogue for light-weight textiles advanced, the fussiness and dimensionality of trimming decreased. The outlines of the dress were quite unbroken by loops of ribbon, puffs and swags of tulle, artificial flowers or gathered furbelows. Delicate trails of naturalistic foliage, or neat geometrical borders, in the lightest embroidery, seem almost finely pencilled on the uneventful surface – as indeed on occasion they were. The London Museum owns an unmade skirt of almost transparent silver silk, on to which is appliquéd a decoration of oval taffeta medallions, each painted with a watercolour picture of playing children, enclosed in an embroidered Greek 'key' patterned frame – analogous to the classical plaques by Wedgwood, which Robert Adam had been setting into furniture for some years past. Another similar surviving example has medallions of paper, printed with engraved designs sewn to its surface.[10]

The plain, close-fitting, undemonstrative clothes of the men were surely neat and spruce enough for George Brummel's most puritanical standards, yet he was still only sixteen, and hardly known. As so often, on examination, supposed initiators prove to be the brilliant exploiters of ideas already under way. The perfect grooming for which Brummel was famed by 1799 (making it into a fetish to mark the 'gentleman') was the apotheosis in dress of the Neo-classical ideals of honesty, integrity, truth, industry and rational seriousness. 'Natural', untrimmed simple fabric, well cut, carefully fitted and constantly brushed; clean linen freshly starched; well cured leather, brilliantly polished; all were to be worn without over-consciousness or impressive display. The English contribution to an international style was brought to a climax.

One of the refugees from the Revolution in France was the German, Niklaus von Heideloff, who had been working in Paris since 1784. He fled to England, and in May 1794 published the first number of his *Gallery of Fashion*. At last England had a publication as elegant and authoritative as anything produced in Paris. The idealized dream-world of the artist was becoming more readily available to a wider public, encouraging higher standards, and giving a certain popular realization to

10 *See Bulletin du Musée Carnavalet* (June, 1966).

the mental image. In the introduction to his second volume in 1795 the artist flatteringly commented:

> In our memory France has given her dresses to other nations: but it was reserved for the Graces of Great Britain to take the lead in Fashion and to show that if they do not surpass, they certainly equal the elegance of the most celebrated Grecian dresses.

With the establishment of the Directory in France in that same year, the country began to settle down. Jacques Louis David, the painter whose classical pictures had provided symbols for the Revolutionaries, who had designed classical uniforms of tunics, togas and Phrygian caps for officers of the state, and classical pageants to celebrate the victory of democracy, now painted the Sériziat family in the first year of the new régime.[11] Except for his revolutionary cockade, Monsieur could pass for an Englishman. The past remains in his still powdered hair, but the plain coat of wool cloth, its turn-over collar and wide lapels developed from those of the English 'little loose-frock'; the buckskin breeches which display his thighs like the smoothly modelled limbs of a classical statue, and the well cut, polished riding-boots, are all entirely modern and 'masculine', in contrast to the totally feminine delicacy of Madame's unfussy muslin. Liberty and equality appear triumphant – but what of antiquity?

It is to be glimpsed among the plates from the charming series, *Costume Parisien*, published by La Mésangère from the 1790s. The relief after the horrors of 1793 to 1795 very naturally found expression in wildness and extremism. The feeling is expressed in these pictures, which are not true fashion plates. (They are records of dress seen; like those of Heideloff 'they are not imaginary but really existing ones'.[12]) All the old rules had been gradually undermined; now chaos had come and almost anything seemed possible. Though by 1797 Robespierre had been dead three years, still a red ribbon round the throat and *ceinture à la Victime* seemed morbidly amusing, particularly when worn with a nonsensical *bonnet à la Jardinière*, or with hair chopped short *à la porc-épic*, like those who had been polled for execution. Yet that particular method of girding a dress had also been used in Ancient Greece to hold the chiton; while the short hair, if more carefully curled, could be re-named *à la Caracalla*. Roman sandals upon bare feet, and a splendidly 'classical' version of the old-fashioned bag-pocket (hung now flamboyantly outside rather than concealed beneath the petticoat), could transform the simple muslin frock into a passable revival of an antique mode. Overtunics and geometric peplums with weights dangling from the corners, were gathered on at a waistline raised to a level immediately below the breasts, and sleeves caught together at intervals with cameos or buttons, provided further classical detail. Bonnets had in general replaced hats, and could conveniently give more than a hint of Minerva's helmet. The shawl, a fashionable accessory since the 1770s, now came into its own, both to increase the 'antique' appearance when well and picturesquely draped, or simply for increased warmth when fashion was demanding unprecedented scantiness of dress. Often expensive and oriental in design, shawls and scarves were also given key-pattern or laurel-wreath borders in

11 Louvre, Paris.

12 For a definition of the fashion-plate, *see* Langley Moore, Doris, *Fashion through Fashion Plates 1770–1970* (London, 1971).

In the 1790s, Roman sandals worn on bare feet and splendidly Classical versions of old-fashioned bag pockets made a passable revival of the antique mode. (From *Costume Parisien*, 1798.)

embroidery or braid. The fabrics used for dress were predominantly in the purity of white, offset by 'natural', 'masculine' colours – stone, bright lapis blue, hot ochre yellow, strong terracotta and dark malachite green. Antiquity was catching up – and with its fancy-dress effects was more than hinting at romance. What dresses now lacked in width they made up for in length, and it was necessary to drape great swathes of fabric over the arms, to reveal artfully the ribbons of classically tied slippers, criss-crossing up the leg. Although by no means meagre, the quantity of material required for a dress had considerably decreased. In 1788, Betsy Sheridan had mentioned that she needed twenty-two yards of poplin for a gown and petticoat. By 1798, Jane Austen was wondering if seven yards would do for her new frock. Although memoirs of the age are crammed with references to 'transparent dresses that leave you certain there is no chemise beneath!'[13] the apparently honest plates in *Costume Parisien* show that the majority wore plenty of fabric in the dress, and that many must have had not only a chemise, but several petticoats, and the addition of a small pad beneath. Even an apparently sleeveless shift, *à la Prêtresse*, is described in the text as being worn over a skin-tight undergarment of knitted flesh-coloured silk which covers the arms right down to the wrists. Bodices certainly were cut incredibly low, but as the sight of the entire upper half of the breasts had been quite familiar for over two centuries it could hardly have come as any shocking revelation. Madame Hamelin, famed for her daring among the more raffish and extreme, is reputed to have walked through Paris bare to the waist. This probably meant something like the dress shown in her portrait by David, in which, although the bodice itself is cut low enough to reveal her nipples, the breasts are fetchingly veiled by an overdress of not quite transparent muslin. Such excesses, however well authenticated, were clearly the exception rather than the rule.

Male dress had settled into a uniform convention of dark coat, light waistcoat and skin-tight breeches or stockinet pantaloons. Just as feminine dress displayed a natural figure for the first time in about four hundred years, so too did masculine dress. The fronts of the coat were cut away, higher and higher, to complement the rising female waistline. The torso and legs were displayed in an unbroken line, from ribcage to calf, while the pantaloons or breeches were made so high in the rise, that they reached almost to the armpits. Waistcoat and breeches, usually light in colour, ideally fitted without a wrinkle, to present the body as nearly 'naturally' as could be acceptably allowed. The charm and simplicity which had resulted from the immense changes for both sexes is beautifully displayed by the Danish Jens Juel in his portrait of the Ryborg family in 1798. But then, curiously to the horror of the majority, grown men who were not peasants were actually to be seen wearing trousers, not nearly so revealing of the natural form. Fashionably, trousers were a logical development from close-fitted pantaloons (which had been themselves simply an extension down on to the lower-leg of form-fitting breeches, giving greater unity and definition to the limb). At the same time, they seem to have been a rare example of a working-class 'fashion'. Traditional wear for sailors, they had been otherwise little used for centuries, until small boys began to be dressed in them after about 1760. In the late

13 Lady Louisa Stuart, *Gleanings from an Old Portfolio*, quoted by Norah Waugh in *The Cut of Women's Clothes* (London, 1968).

eighteenth century the requirement of a strong visual proletarian opposition to established form appears to have prompted a wider adoption by adults of this obviously utilitarian garment. Identification with the oppressed was a sufficient reason for its vogue among intellectuals. The fact that trousers were both different and defiant was reason enough for them to acquire *cachet* in advanced fashionable circles. It is probably a pure coincidence that the young Romantics, who were dealing the first fundamental blow to the classical Latin tradition of European civilization since Rome was invaded by northern barbarians, should, like those barbarians, have chosen to wear trousers – but then the coincidence is there.

For the conservative in every country the horrors were increasing. Forces, which for more than half a century had been building to a climax, broke and retreated, leaving behind strangely assorted débris. The progressive, permissive, mainly young and generally opportunist people, who led society in France during the Directory and the Consulate, were not sartorial innovators. The Incredibles and the Marvellous Ones contributed almost nothing new – they simply carried existing tendencies to the point of caricature by an enthusiastic overstatement. While Brummel preached cleanliness and neatness in London, there was a defiant minority cult of slovenly and dirty dressing in Paris, but this was the final stage of a long process of liberation. The one original contribution made by the lunatic fringe in the 1790s was its experimentation with a new form of coat – the 'frock-coat' – with a closed front and skirts cut evenly all round. This daring garment for the young and adventurous paradoxically gained rapid respectability during the following century. The recently achieved liberty in dress was soon eroded as a great deal of padding began to be added to the high rolling collar of this coat, and an immense stock, rather like a bandage, clamped the even higher starched points of the shirt-collar against each cheek. By 1802 newer ideals had come forward.

In that year Napoléon Bonaparte was elected First Consul for life. He was pictured in his neat scarlet uniform decorated with a Greek honeysuckle border, embroidered in gold: clear, linear, mechanical and unfussy. That classical embroidery strikes the last note of the antiquity for men which David had attempted to revive for formal wear in 1793 and which continued to make the Council of Five Hundred look ridiculous in togas in 1796. The Revolution was over and it was time to settle down. Exaggeration and sloppiness in dress had served their purpose. In a caricature from a rare German magazine of 1803 the messy young man of 1802 with dishevelled hair and clothes at once too tight and too loose, turns from his dressing-table towards the new year, and is miraculously transformed into an old-fashioned neatness and respectability. Janus is shown as fettered by the Mode.

Although in 1803 women's dress was still high-waisted, clinging, and lavishly trained, the purity of classical simplicity was passing. A puffing of the sleeves and the addition of softly gathered frills at throat, wrists and hems introduced a fussier effect. Now that the aristocratic tradition had been completely undermined a more middle-class and distinctly more romantic ideal of womanhood was in competition with libertarian principles. Sense was giving way to sensibility.

One contribution from the 'lunatic fringe' in the 1790s was their experimentation with new forms of the frock-coat, such as one with a closed front and a skirt cut evenly all round. (Based on the *Incroyable* by Carle Vernet, late 1790s.)

In 1804, Napoléon proclaimed himself Emperor, and his coronation robes mixed all the splendours of Byzantium with Gothic tradition and sixteenth-century fashion, in a truly modern and romantic display of grandeur. Great panache and sheer vulgarity were equally combined. In the robes designed by the artist Isabey for Empress Josephine and the Bonaparte sisters, a wired, standing 'Medici' collar of lace, and puffed and slashed sleeves of sixteenth-century derivation, made long enough in the medieval manner to cover the hand to the first knuckle, were combined with the high-waisted dress of classical inspiration. Appropriately realized in thick satin and heavy velvet, the sumptuous dresses were thickly encrusted with glittering embroidery in metal strip and edged with deep gold fringes. The classically dressed hair was bound by a low-placed 'antique' bandeau carried out in flashing eighteenth-century faceted gem stones. The 'Empire' style, a mixture of many borrowed themes, had been defined.

Although many light and transparent fabrics continued in high favour, they were worn, in the newly respectable days, over underskirts of coloured satin instead of pink silk tights, and were mixed with more opulent silks and velvet. For daily wear, the heavy metallic embroidery correct for court dress was replaced by a renewed riot of 'feminine' trimmings. Artificial roses, convolvulus flowers and leaves, hyacinths, garlands of myrtle and multicoloured feathers from exotic paroquets were among the many fancies devised by the dressmakers and haberdashers. Once started, the new elaboration continued as Romanticism finally won the day over Neo-classicism. The author of *Bath Characters or Sketches from Life* (1808) must have appeared very old-fashioned with his complaint about girls from eight to eighteen as 'naked as Titian's Venus, their chemise and petticoat long discarded and the most decently dressed not able to boast of more than half a dozen yards of muslin to cover her', for the really uncovered phase was well passed. Even Thomas Hope's *Costume of the Ancients* published in 1809 was too late to be influential on any but the more conservatively unimaginative dressmakers.

Napoléon's military dictatorship, a romantic attempt to reverse a natural evolution, very properly proved to be the heyday of uniformed splendour. Protection and utility had been the principal considerations for soldiers in the past, but now, while civilian wear had become progressively more rational, armies decked themselves in the most incredibly brilliant and inconvenient fantasies. It seems that in an apprehensive reaction, age-old instincts and traditions rallied in a final outburst of unequivocally masculine display before new principles could be totally accepted. Miles of gold and silver thread were consumed in the decoration of multicoloured uniforms, now as tightly fitted and rigidly uncomfortable as any sixteenth-century doublet and hose. At the same time, the various members of the Bonaparte family installed as monarchs over half of Europe seized the opportunity to invent even more romantic and elaborate fancy dresses for ceremonial moments – combing the past for inspiration, just as women were looking back for ideas to provide details for *their* dress. A certain swaggering flashiness and exaggeration of effect soon began to be reflected from the theatricality of uniforms on to the latest clothing for civilian men. By 1814, Brummell's short reign was over.

Janus fettered by the mode.
From *Charis* magazine, Leipzig,
1803.

His rigorous standards, only ever suited to the temperament of a dedicated minority, had probably always been more an ideal than an actuality, and now that the Neo-classical spirit was yielding to a more complete Romanticism, these began to be undermined by overstatement. Thomas

Far left and above
The tendency for the Neo-classical spirit to yield to a more complete romanticism is seen in Horace Vernet's gentle caricatures of 1814, entitled *Incroyable et Merveilleuse*.

Left
Between 1805 and 1814, women's dress changed little, although the skirt became neatly gored into a flare, with the fullness concentrated at the back. A fullness at the sleevehead kept balance with the widening hem. (From *Costume Parisien*, 1813.)

Moore's satirical *Journal of Sir Valentine Sleek* (1818), forms an apt accompaniment to Horace Vernet's gentle caricatures of 1814 to illustrate the point:

> My pigeon breasts, and padded sleeves,
> Made my whole front en militaire
> . . . By their aid a youth receives
> The approbation of the Fair.

> . . . But as the lily grac'd my cheek,
> I graced the lily with the rose,
> And though my nerves were very weak
> Pierre huddled on my ball-room clothes.
> Cork pumps, false calves, high collar – stays
> That Exquisites with rapture view;
> (Which elegance their shape displays)
> And fashionable wig – quite new.

Paradoxically this feminine armoury resulted in an appearance of distinctive masculinity.

Between 1805 and 1814 women's dress evolved very slowly, and was basically little changed. The skirt, shortened to instep or ankle-length, had been more neatly gored to flare into a smooth cone, all fullness concentrated at the back. Fullness at the sleeve-head kept a balance with the widening hem. But though distinctly smarter, the appearance was gentle and undemonstrative. After the Bourbon Restoration of 1814, English women endorsed the Parisian retention of the highest waistline, and their own appalling wartime equivocation was at an end.

In 1815 most of fashionable Europe gathered in Vienna for the Congress where Prince Metternich organized a series of brilliant balls and receptions, at which the new gored skirts (their shortened hems held out by deep borders of trimming in which ribbons, roses, bouffant puffs and pleated frills of tulle were mixed) proved admirably suited to that 'riotous german dance of modern invention' – the waltz – a very late flowering of liberty.

> Hot from the hand promiscuously applied
> Round the slight waist or down the glowing side;
> Where were the rapture then to clasp the form
> From this lewd grasp and lawless contact warm?

enquired Lord Byron in his poem, *The Waltz*, but protest was useless. The insidious, insistent 'Imperial Waltz, imported from the Rhine' began its long reign over the ballrooms and all Europe was soon dancing to the music of Beethoven, Lanner and Gung'l; Vienna established a claim to be a rival to Paris as a city of Pleasure *par excellence*. Victory seemed complete, and liberty and equality pranced away in three-four time:

> Thee fashion hails – from countesses to queens
> And maids and valets waltz behind the scenes;

Wide and more wide the witching circle spreads,
And turns – if nothing else – at least our heads;
With thee e'en clumsy cits attempt to bounce,
And cockneys practice what they can't pronounce.

But while Congress waltzed, Napoléon had landed in France again, and all those splendid uniforms, the acme of glorious military and masculine magnificence were off to be torn to pieces, amid the romantic heroism, the filth, mud and blood of Waterloo.

From Romance to Materialism

She sate absorbed in a train of contemplations, dimly defined, but infinitely delightful: emotions rather than thoughts, which attention would have utterly dissipated, if it had paused to seize their images.

Thomas Love Peacock

Melincourt 1817

The aftermath of the devastating Napoleonic Wars left depression throughout Europe. Theoretically the waltzing continued, but in reality there was a general lassitude. In England, the old, conservative middle classes of the professions, banking and commerce, had been augmented by more recently wealthy industrial families; and on the Continent, by those of a new military nobility created by the Empire, together with army contractors, and many other speculators whose money was made during the years of crisis. These were the inheritors of power, once exclusively aristocratic. They continued until at least 1820 to dress in a modified version of French court-style, now marked by a sober excellence rather than extravagant luxury. France and England had imposed between them an equality of appearance over the entire Continent, for all 'polite society'. This term had come to include far greater variations in birth, breeding, wealth and education, than could ever have been conceivable before. From the Baltic to the Bay of Biscay, from Stockholm to Palermo, women of even the most modest means, who had any pretension to style, looked automatically to Paris, and men to London. Suits of solemn black were certainly not yet entirely customary, but gradually they became the only acceptable wear for 'respectable' men – and more men were aspiring to respectability. Women only slightly modified the once gracefully clinging, classically inspired line (in principle unbroken for over seventeen

Headpiece for *Master Humphrey's Clock* by artist George Cattermole. (Published in 1840.)

145

years) by loading its less yielding surface with light but elaborate decoration and sixteenth-century detail. Millinery, confined entirely to the form of the enclosing bonnet, provided the most inventive, spontaneous and contemporary expression, to herald a freshly emerging epoch in dress. During the 1820s a quite new image was evolved from material to hand. Inch by inch, the waist was lowered towards its natural position, while sleeve-heads and skirt hems were given greater emphasis from increasing volume and concentrated ornament. A last vestige of the old 'Empire line' was frequently retained in the arrangement of a horizontally-pleated, corsage-decoration, high across the bust. The return to a normal demarcation of the waist led inevitably to returning restriction by the stays, but, as in earlier instances, recent experience was not totally abandoned. No corset in the nineteenth century, however restrictive, was ever to suppress the breasts or convert the torso into an abstract cone. The eighteenth-century Revolution had permanently restored to women a woman's shape. It might be exaggerated, abstracted and frequently adjusted, but always the abstraction would be based on curves, in an hourglass rather than an ice-cream cornet silhouette. Trousers for men had lost their unsettling revolutionary connotations (at least by 1807), to acquire a certain smart *cachet*; and from 1820 many innovations in the cut of this garment allowed a wide selection of very varied shapes although its full social standing was only gradually achieved.

During the years of the Revolution, and the Napoleonic Empire, the traditional role of the artist as servant to an informed aristocratic patronage had come under the same reconsideration as every other aspect of the former social order. That he possessed the absolute right to a private expression of his personal sensitivity and imagination, became a firmly held belief. Untrammelled practice of that right appeared the only honest and honourable course. The whole duty of the artist was to discover his heart, and to explore his soul, by any and by every means he could. He must experience to the full every possibility that life could offer; examine his reactions; and record them with uncontrolled emotion. Passionate involvement seems a logical reaction to the rational detachment encouraged by the Age of Reason. Yet the roots of Romanticism lie deep in the eighteenth century. Both the Rococo style and Neo-classical opposition to it were in some respects earlier, less committed manifestations of that later mood. The official art and decoration of the Empire had taken the clarity, the hard-edged purity and precision, the sparseness of ornamentation in the revolutionary work of the painter David, and made these things its own. It had adopted the forms of the carefully reconstructed antique accessories and furniture which that artist had commissioned from the cabinet-maker Jacob, and had inflated them to the superhuman proportions its megalomania required. This weighty and imposingly romantic view of antiquity, in which Piranesi's Roman magnificence of scale combined with the uncomplicated purity attributed by Winckelmann to Greece, was inherited by Biedermeier Europe. By economically dispensing with most of the extravagance of applied metallic ornament, while comfortably thickening the upholstery and adding extra layers to the drapery, it presented a worthy impression of sound return for every penny spent. The Napoleonic régime had been insufficiently confident aesthetically to encourage

In the early nineteenth century, the once Classical line was broken, by cluttering surfaces with light, elaborate decoration, and sixteenth-century detail. (*Les Garnitures* from *Incroyable et Merveilleuse* by Horace Vernet, 1814.)

any originality of expression. Its official endorsement of the Neo-classicism naturally evolved as a part of the nationalistic, revolutionary process was given added weight by the public display in Paris of famed Classical works, upon which Renaissance traditions had depended. These were brought by the Emperor as plunder from the despoiled dominions over which his family ruled. The successors of the Empire, even less confident amid the ruins of all recognizable order, clung to the official art they had inherited as their one security and established it as academic practice for the next half century.

This was the background against which Romanticism in its narrower sense developed. The intellectuals and artists of the eighteenth century had faced reality and tried to master it. The young Romantics of the immediate post-Revolutionary years faced reality and felt themselves to be at its mercy. Gripped by nervous tension, they saw Nature as truly awe-full and their utter independence of all former authority as appalling. Terror, frustration, and a firm resolve not to surrender to the limitations which the official classicism seemed to imply, called on a passionate heroism of mind. An antidote to reality was available in flights of imaginative fantasy, not towards the chilling predictability of the too familiar world of antiquity, but to the romance and chivalry of an imaginary Middle Ages. So the paradoxes multiply. William Blake's unprecedented burning visions were realized in the coolest Neo-classical technique: that linear style considered the most 'pure and natural'. John Keats took the 'Attic shape' of a classical subject for his *Ode on a Grecian Urn* and apostrophized it in terms of dream and 'Wild ecstasy'. De Loutherbourg had pictured the modern reality of the 'dark satanic mills' of *Coalbrookdale by Night* with all the spectacular excitement he would lavish on the eruption of Vesuvius or that a Gothic artist could have brought to the portrayal of Hell's Mouth.[1]

The principal formative control upon the arts until the eighteenth century had been that of enlightened patronage, mainly from the church, the aristocracy or the state. With the important exception of the Netherlands, merchants and bankers had not been conspicuous for private encouragement of the visual arts. Although the economic power of the new middle classes now provided them the opportunity to indulge their tastes in this field, they played their part, not so much as direct commissioning patrons, but as the purchasers of the more personal products of artists now independent of the earlier system of control – who had been freed to fight and starve if their expression was not apposite, or to accommodate themselves to the outlook of an important group, having no solid background of aesthetic understanding. Standards for the sixteenth and seventeenth centuries had been set by architecture, sculpture, and a style of painting which illusionistically related to the two – a most natural expression of the Italian interest in form. Decorative arts, the spontaneous product of French interest in line and pattern, had dominated the eighteenth century. Literature, music and philosophy were to take the lead during the first half of the nineteenth. These forms of expression were most suited to temperaments consistently romantic: literature to England; music and philosophy to Germany. They were also expressions which could be made most readily available to the greatest numbers, and

1   De Loutherbourg,
Coalbrookdale by Night
(Science Museum, London).

which could therefore be the most widely influential in the creation of a mental climate for 'contemplations, dimly defined, but infinitely delightful'. Literature was one art in which the middle classes had been able to participate for centuries, and upon which their ethos and outlook had begun to have an important effect by 1740. Music had always been an accomplishment to prove the refinement of the practitioner. The introduction of the 'pianoforte', an instrument with a far greater range of colourful expression than any so far domestically available, provided talent as well as genius with the opportunity for immediate stimulus to reverie, dream and melancholy, or to fiery passion. The other arts could only serve to illustrate evocative themes.

Once the standards of the middle classes had taken their effect on all levels of society, men ideally were *gentlemen*. In any event they were unmistakably male. Women were no longer really women. At the least they were *ladies*, and at the best fairies or angels. There was nothing new about likening a woman to an angel. It is not the angelic comparison itself which is so significant in the nineteenth century, but the nineteenth century's concept of the angels. In the Middle Ages, angels were carved or painted to look awe-inspiring and completely devoid of sexuality. By the Renaissance, when Man was the measure of all things, angels developed a definite tendency towards masculinity. During the eighteenth century, androgynous qualities gradually increased, and by the nineteenth, angels were unmistakably 'painted fair' to look like women. Any true spirituality was gone – angels were earthbound and sentimental. When not vapid, they were grave, gracious, kind or understanding; seldom wrathful or avenging. Angels had acquired all the qualities of the perfect lady – and ladies aspired to be indistinguishable from angels – or men chose to believe them so. In lighter moments, they might be fairies – a cross between a sprightly wayward child and a mischievous wood-nymph. For the male, whether he accepted or conflicted with modern technology, industry and science, woman had come to personify both the Soul, and the Untamed Spirit of Nature:

In the early nineteenth century angels were unmistakably 'painted fair' to look like women. But true spirituality had gone. These angels were sentimental and vapid.

> Oh woman! in our hours of ease
> Uncertain, coy, and hard to please,
> And variable as the shade
> By the light quivering aspen made;
> When pain and anguish wring the brow
> A ministering angel thou.

So proclaimed Walter Scott in *Marmion* (1808). By 1830, his works were fashionable reading for all Europe. The idea of the ultra-feminine woman had been a long time forming. She had appeared quite clearly in Richardson's virtuous *Pamela* in 1740. During the later eighteenth century, Rousseau's Julie in *La Nouvelle Héloïse*, and Lotte, the heroine of Goethe's *The Sorrows of Werther*, developed her possibility. During the early nineteenth century, the full flood of the Romantic Movement, with its passion, its reviving medievalism and dreams of chivalry, crystallized the whole conception. In 1804, Wordsworth wrote rapturously of the new ideal:

The nineteenth century saw a
complete reversal in colouring,
when the romantic spirit
delighted in pale, opalescent
colours, and women became
fair, fragile, creatures, of an
almost angelic delicacy.
(Marie Taglioni in *La Sylphide*
by A. C. Chalon, published
1845; *Petit Courier des Dames*,
July, 1833.)

She was a Phantom of delight
When first she gleam'd upon my sight;
A lovely apparition, sent
To be a moment's ornament;
Her eyes as stars of twilight fair;
Like twilights' too, her dusky hair;
But all things else about her drawn
From May-time and the cheerful dawn;
A dancing shape, an image gay,
To haunt, to startle, and waylay.
I saw her upon nearer view,
A Spirit, yet a Woman too!
Her household motions light and free,
And steps of virgin-liberty;
A countenance in which did meet
Sweet records, promises as sweet;
A creature not too bright or good
For human nature's daily food;
For transient sorrows, simple wiles,
Praise, blame, love, kisses, tears and smiles.
And now I see with eye serene
The very pulse of the machine;
A being breathing thoughtful breath,
A traveller between life and death;
The reason firm, the temperate will,
Endurance, foresight, strength and skill;
A perfect Woman, nobly plann'd,
To warn, to comfort, and command;
And yet a Spirit still, and bright
With something of angelic light.

Long before 1830 such a picture had changed from an individual's romantic dream into a fashionable ideal. Throughout the first half of the nineteenth century, the double image of the two aspects of this ideal woman, angel and fairy – the soul and the spirit of nature – made repeated appearances in the formative force of popular literature. The natural sense and sensibility of Jane Austen's Elinor and Marianne, appear again more artificially cultivated in the grave, self-effacing comfort offered to David Copperfield by Agnes Wickfield when he is deprived of the drooping fragility and quivering incompetence of Dora Spenlow. As late as 1860 the fay beauty of Laura Fairlie is constantly supported by the selfless ministering of the ugly Marion Halcombe, who in the closing chapter of Wilkie Collins' *The Woman in White*, is referred to as 'the good angel in our lives'. The importance of such creations upon the tone of the age cannot be underestimated. It must be remembered that English novels were as widely read abroad as at home. In daily life many women temperamentally unsuited to play *either* role, might, like Florence Nightingale, by determined independence achieve the title of heroine in fact. But in fiction, women of independent determination could never play the lead.

They played supporting parts – either comic, like Betsy Trotwood; or tragic, like Lady Deadlock or the second Mrs Dombey. It was not until late in the 1860s that such women assumed the lead in literature. Bella Wilfer in *Our Mutual Friend* or Gwendolen Harleth in *Daniel Deronda* are already figures of a very different age. For the first fifty years of the nineteenth century, while the whole aim of fashionable dress was to create an idealized youthful fragile prettiness, those women who were large, brisk and middle-aged often had no alternative but to appear comic or tragic, should they be inclined to comply with the mode. A most important contribution towards the essential image was made by the ballet, whose stars could well stand as a symbol for the age.

Here Woman had become a spirit indeed, so light that she seemed to fly. In the seventeenth century, ballet had been an almost exclusively masculine preserve. Inroads were made by female dancers in the eighteenth century, and Carmogo was the first woman to perform an *entrechat*, a movement formerly reserved for men alone. By the nineteenth century, the showy male role was considerably reduced, frequently to that of *porteur*, simply to support the ballerina at some particularly difficult balance as she assumed more spectacular effects. Exactly when the dancer first rose on to her points seems to be uncertain – probably during the 1820s. The developing fashionable ideal had evolved a very narrow light, flexible, heelless slipper, constructed with a sole slightly too small for the wearer. The fabric of the upper, wrapping closely around the foot, compressed the bones together and encouraged them into the slender elongated elegance demanded by the mode. It was in this ordinary smart slipper of the day, wearing an ethereal muslin ball-gown that in 1832 'La Sylphide' Taglioni, with tiny gauze wings sprouting at her waist, rose into the air, poised upon one unblocked toe to pluck a bird's nest playfully from a tree. The effect was complete – the spirit of the period personified. In 1841, *Giselle* appeared to add a last inimitable touch – the wronged woman, sent mad by the thoughtless selfish man; her spirit turned to a fluttering 'Willy' redeeming him for love. It is worth considering that this incredible delicacy of effect was achieved only by an almost superhuman strength and discipline. Of all the brilliant ballerinas who, curiously, so abounded in the early nineteenth century to give force to an ideal image, two lived to be eighty, and one survived to ninety-two.

This fashionable ideal required of course a complementary male counterpart. By the 1840s, the female novelist, no longer a rarity, was working to provide it.

Half reclined on a couch appeared Mr. Rochester . . . The fire shone full on his face. I knew my traveller, with his broad and jetty eyebrows, his square forehead, made squarer by the horizontal sweep of his black hair.

I recognised his decisive nose, more remarkable for character than beauty; his full nostrils, denoting, I thought, choler; his grim mouth, chin and jaw – yes, all three were very grim, and no mistake. His shape, now divested of cloak, I perceived harmonised in squareness with his physiognomy. I suppose it was a good figure in the athletic sense of the term – broad chested and thin-flanked, though neither tall nor graceful.

Mr. Rochester must have been aware of the entrance of Mrs. Fairfax and myself; but it appeared he was not in the mood to notice us, for he never lifted his head as we approached.[2]

If Wordsworth's view of Woman had been an impossible masculine idealization of femininity, too good to be true, then the portrait of Mr Rochester is surely a feverishly feminine view of masterful masculinity. But the two extremes were needed to preserve a balance. The aristocratic ideals of the past had allowed that Woman although inferior in imagination and physical strength was at least of the same genus as Man, and could share much with him. For the romantic bourgeois standards prevailing throughout Europe before 1830, men and women were at absolute opposite poles. Like the figures in a weather-house, the woman all angelic goodness, sunshine and light, the man all stormy animal passion and fire, they stood at each end of an inflexible bar, firmly fixed in position by popular belief and morality. An inhibited lack of frankness on the subject of sex led to an overheated complexity seething below the surface. It gave a distinct eroticism to even quite innocent subjects, and as the ideas and ideals of the time were made manifest in fashionable dress and fashionable behaviour, a thinly veiled eroticism is evident in both.

Between 1830, when the romantic ideal had fully emerged, and 1860, when it had passed its climax and was beginning to disintegrate, there was a most logical development in fashionable figures. Women changed gradually from a timid, blushing youthfulness, all 'sheep's-eyes' and breathless calf-love, to a complete assurance and unequivocal maturity. The frivolities of the thirties gave place to the slender seriousness of the forties, which in its turn was transformed into the expansive graciousness of the fifties. It is possible to see the ideal ageing from year to year, filling out and gaining confidence as the mid-century approached, becoming worldly and materialistic, and seeing its youthful romanticism as nothing but childish nonsense. The delicate, dizzy, bottle-shouldered child-bride Dora did not in reality die, but was transformed by the years into the opulently bosomed, commanding Mrs Proudie, with a mind of her own, the undisputed dictator of the social graces. The ardent, inexperienced David Copperfield developed into the massively solid Pater of a large Familia, in whom the puritan virtue of the Prince Consort could all too easily merge into the sinister sadistics of a John Jasper, or the private violence of Sir Percival Glyde. The dashing elegance of the dandy D'Orsay gradually thickened and coarsened into the 'heavy-swell' of Lord Dundreary. If the fashion-plate ideal of 1840 was aged between seventeen and twenty, this had advanced by 1860 to thirty or thirty-five.

The quiet Biedermeier tranquillity, which fostered dreams of romance, tinged with a delicate passion never too much uncontrolled, dominated the 1820s. It was a time of adjustment for the middle classes to their new position as social arbiters, and in dress, as in architecture and decoration, there was frequently an uninhibited, showy vulgarity, not yet tamed. For women, their personification of the spirit of nature – uncertain, coy, and hard to please – was in the ascendant. By the late twenties there was a great deal of childish nonsense, all bounce and immaturity. Neat, child-

2 Brontë, Charlotte, *Jane Eyre*, 1847.

During the late 1820s, a great deal of childish nonsense was seen in dress. (From *Wiener Moden*, 1826.)

Any accusation of lack of colour, variety or dullness in male dress is speedily disproved by reference to Count d'Orsay, Charles Dickens or Disraeli. 'Divers boys of from fifteen to twenty-one years of age, throw back their coats and turn up their wristbands, after the portraits of Count D'Orsay', wrote Dickens in *Sketches by Boz*, 1836.

like, belted waists; ankle-length skirts; nodding plumes, fluttering ribbons, buoyant sleeves, bubbling 'sausage' curls all gave a general air of great activity and constant skipping motion. The exaggerated width of bonnet brims, and the increased size of sleeves, overlaid by emphasizing epaulettes, while diminishing the apparent circumference of the waist, made an impression of clothes too large for the tiny figure. The suggestion is that of a small girl wearing her mother's dress. Balloon-sleeves, carried beyond the limit of logic, became so large before 1832 that sleeve-pillows, filled with down, were required for their support. But from this point of climax, deflation began almost at once. First, the removal of the pillows allowed the fullness of the sleeve to droop towards the elbow. This had the effect of continuing the long, sloping line of the shoulder, principally produced by the very low setting-in of the sleeve. At the same time the open brim of the bonnet, although still generously wide, closed in around the face. By 1834 the bounciness of the late twenties was being subdued. The little girls began to grow up.

Men retained something of the military, cocky swagger, which had resulted from the masculine display indulged by the romanticism of the Napoleonic era. The throwing-open of the coat gave an air of carelessness and irresponsibility. Strong, bright colours, and the strange contrast of top-heavy hats above the shrunken look of tight, ankle-length pantaloons is suggestive of a precocious little boy. There has been a general impression that masculine dress became so dull after the opening years of the nineteenth century that it is not worth mentioning. All attention has tended to concentrate on the very obvious variety of women's dress, and male clothing has been dismissed as uninteresting and uniform. Throughout the century, however, there was considerable colour and infinite variety in the forms and types of garments, even though the general effect is somewhat self-effacing. To suggest that men had made a great renunciation, giving up clothes that depended upon obvious sex-appeal is patently untrue when they are seen to provide the necessary complement to an exaggerated femininity. We must not try to find our own ideas of sexual attractiveness expressed by earlier epochs. Indeed it could be claimed that, as with women's dress, the clothing of the nineteenth century was the first in history to place sexual appeal prominently before all other consideration. It cannot be without significance that an age which had, by dress and manners, so effectively separated men from women, should close with the formulation of sexual psychology. Any accusations that a retiring lack of colour, lack of variety and dullness were general to the century is speedily disproved by reference to Count D'Orsay, Dickens and Disraeli. They were not alone, but much admired and imitated by many, if despised by some. Although the composition of the fashionable figure in the thirties was built-up from opulent, feminine-looking curves, its effect is far from effeminate. The breadth across the shoulder, given by the great rolling, padded collar and wide lapels, emphasizes the narrowness of waist and hips, and concentrates all attention on the legs. These were encased, as Jane Carlyle described, in 'invisible inexpressibles, skin-coloured and fitting like a glove'. Constant references to cravats of sky-blue satin or waistcoats in green and purple stripes; yards of gold chain; lemon gloves; diamond-studs; coloured stones and enamelled boots, are hardly suggestive of a retiring ideal. Fashion plates indicate such items as a damson coloured opera-cloak, lined with flame-silk and trimmed with violet cord; or an ankle-length dressing-gown in scarlet damask, with Turkish slippers in ochre morocco. George Brummel's puritanical Neo-classic standards had rapidly declined, and an aggressively Romantic masculine display was to remain very evident until the late 1850s. In the thirties the general effect of swaggering self-confidence and colour is youthful. Light and brisk, it is expressive of a dancing animation. But raffish splendour was waning a little by 1840. Masculinity was less flashily displayed.

20 Septembre 1844.

2044.

Modes de Paris.

Romanticism suggested that the newly emerging, softer feminine ideal – the angel in the house – required a less bold, more serious approach. Still firm, but gentler handling was called for. Men were not to be subdued, but became deferential. By 1837, the hems of women's skirts had dropped again to floor length. The bounce was quite gone, replaced by a sensitive fragility. The last vestige of the expansive sleeve hung modestly about the wrist, the upper section above the elbow encircled only by a few delicate frills or close set gauging. The corset was cut much longer in the waist, and its curves were drawn out into shallow, sinuous lines which moulded the bust tightly like the calix of a still-closed flower. By 1840, the bonnet, its brim much reduced, closed closely round the face in a narrow inverted U. The hair, centrally parted, was plastered down with 'Bandoline', seeming painted on to the perfect narrow oval of the head, and from ear-level it dripped into long forlorn 'spaniel' ringlets. Timidity and helpless resignation were emphasized by the binding of the arms to the body in a shawl; exactly placed about the points of the shoulders, it muffled the figure and carried the eye down into the billowing skirts without a break. The entire composition was built up from shallow elliptical curves. Passing over the smoothly polished hair, the gaze slides down the drooping shoulders, then slithers the length of the elongated torso, over the gently padded hips and on to the heavily dragging skirts, which were supported by a burden of innumerable petticoats. The plump, cheeky little girls of the preceding years had been transformed into enervated, shy, serious adolescents, slender and gazelle-like.

The dullest decade in the history of feminine dress began in 1840. An insipid mediocrity characterized an entirely middle-class epoch. Nowhere in Europe was there the prime necessity for dynamic fashion – a splendid and extravagant court, or some alternative social centre to set the pace. The best-dressed woman in Paris was said to be Marie Duplessis, the real-life original for Marguerite Gautier, Dumas' 'Lady of the Camelias'. This archetype of all golden-hearted whores always behaved and looked like an angelic perfect lady, however she earned her keep. Describing the late forties, when his father arrived in the French capital as a modest draper's assistant, M. Jean Worth wrote:

> When M. Worth came to Paris it was difficult to believe that the gay city had ever been the centre of a brilliant court. Each lady boasted of a mantle or rotande, a couple of silk gowns made with a view to hard and prolonged wear, and perhaps a cashmere shawl presented to her on her marriage. The most expensive trimming in those days cost four francs a yard, and in all Paris there was only one dressmaker who provided both material and façon; in other words everyone but Mme. Roger's clients bought their own material and then took it to some little dressmaker to be made up.[3]

Hardly an atmosphere to encourage invention or emulation. If proof should be required that fashion in dress is as fluctuating in its motivation as in its forms, it is provided by the 'Year of Revolutions', 1848. In the eighteenth century, clothing had played a most notable part in the creation of an atmosphere of total revolt against every aspect of decaying social

The period from 1840 to 1850 was the dullest decade in feminine dress, which demonstrated an insipid mediocrity. (From *Petit Courier des Dames*, 1844.)

3 'La Maison Worth' – An interview with M. Jean Worth, by Marie A. Belloc, published in *The Lady's Realm*, 1896.

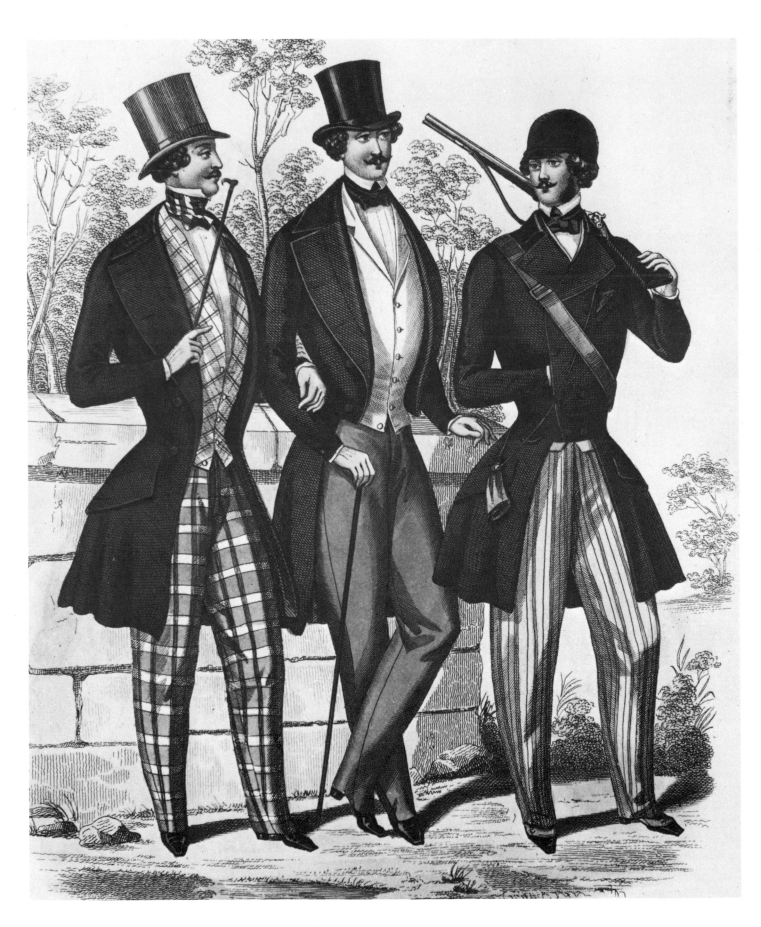

order. Intense nationalism, one aspect of the Romantic spirit, which resulted in the revolutionary outbreaks of the 1840s, left fashionable dresses quite untouched. The interest in dress was concerned mainly with the domestic reassessment of the position of male and female in society. By 1844 the angelic woman had acquired a rather heavier masculine companion. The dashing lightness, exemplified by D'Orsay, had thickened and gained weight. A dropped waistline for the coat gave a bigger, more solid-looking torso. Fuller trousers suggested sturdier, less shapely legs. The highly favoured, boldly checked cloths, seem best suited to the race-track or other sporty masculine pursuits. If there was a double image for the female, this had a masculine equivalent too. One face showed a dependable sobriety in the high-principled leader of the family, with a strong arm for support; the other, that racketiness of younger sons out upon the spree; the allowable sowing of 'wild-oats' which made men so 'different' and able 'to deal with things'. If a woman's place was at this time definitely in the home, then many a man had an existence outside it – which, like his trousers, was 'inexpressible' or 'unmentionable'. There was a half-world, in which women who were *not* ladies played a prominent part; a world which women who *were* ladies pretended did not even exist.

But ladies were learning and maturing. By 1851 the insipidity of the forties was turning to a growing opulence and certainty. The drawn-out, shallow, enervated curves gradually broadened into a more definite roundness. The bonnet widened at the side into a full-circle instead of forming a narrow vertical hoop. The hair, still centrally parted and smoothly brushed, acquired width, being turned under, to stand out from the head above the ears, in broad, flat, ribbon-like loops. Skirts expanded to even greater width over additional petticoats of horsehair cloth or quilted down, and with the extra optical illusion of continuously repeated horizontal trimming added in the form of applied bands, or dimensional flounces. By 1856 the trimming of the bodice was more frequently applied in a generous sweep across the bust, than placed vertically to emphasize a narrow waist. A more ample, graciously matronly woman had taken the place of the sickly angelic doll of the forties. Those pretty adolescents, being made of far stronger stuff than they pretended, survived the horrors of the marriage-bed to reveal an iron hand within a velvet glove. From this time on, woman was the dominant sex in the domestic field, and in all matters of social life and etiquette. The calm angelic presence had become the magisterial hostess, mother of a large family and mistress of a larger staff, both of whom she ruled with a gentle, unmistakable authority. Advised by Mrs Beeton, she held 'the reins with a tight, firm hand, never parting with, but seldom using, the whip'. The arbiter of manners and of taste, she *made* the rules, and by fair means or by foul, saw that they were obeyed. A woman no longer drooped hesitantly. Her carriage was upright and she looked her adversary directly in the eye, since her vision was no longer blinkered by her bonnet, which she now wore far back, resting on a thick *chignon*. The artist Ingres, still working in the chilling clarity of Neo-classical technique (now termed Academic) painted Mme Moitesseier in 1851[4] and again in 1856.[5] There is nothing fragile or angelic about the smoothly well-fed face of this lady,

In the 1840s, men favoured highly those large, boldly checked cloths which seem more suited to the racecourse than the town street. (From *Petit Courier des Dames*, 1844.)

4   National Gallery, Washington.

5   National Gallery, London.

By the 1850s, a woman no longer drooped angelically – her carriage was upright, and she looked her adversary directly in the eye. (From *English Women's Domestic Magazine*, 1861.)

6   Dickens, Charles, *Our Mutal Friend*, 1864.

who could well be the fictional Mrs Veneering,[6] that upstart lady from London. Women were really coming down to earth to take their fair share of the materialism which masculinity had industriously provided. The female dress of the forties suggests perhaps the tremulous playing of a wistful Chopin nocturne on a solitary piano, but by the sixties the full surge of a Brahmsian orchestra would provide a more apt accompaniment. As women became socially more powerful, so they increased physically in volume, being on occasion literally inflated by penumatic tubes. Before 1860 the skirt had reached its maximum possible size, spread over a wire cage, and a woman covered a vast area of ground. The delicate shot-silks in opalescent colours so favoured by the serious forties, gave place to a harsher clarity and brilliance. It has been suggested that the garish colours used for dress during the mid-century were due to the invention in 1860 of aniline dyes, but the onus may well be another way. Such colours had been appearing in the paintings of the Pre-Raphaelite Brotherhood and those of other artists earlier than the fifties, helping to stimulate a desire for much more brilliant effects. In contrast to the hesitancy which had first appeared in dress late in the thirties, the dresses of the fifties have a self-confident, overpowering vulgarity. Now the spirit of expansion was in the air. The trumpets of the Second Empire sounded in 1852. Louis

Napoléon Bonaparte was proclaimed Emperor Napoléon III. Europe once more had a focus for fashion: a wildly extravagant if parvenu court (which as an economic policy encouraged competitive display of luxury) set in a city rapidly rebuilt in the most modern manner.

The flamboyant society of the French capital was chronicled in 1854 by Gustave Doré in *La Ménagerie Parisienne*. Here the 'Lionesses', the new generation of bolder more magnificent women, are shown flashing past in landaus, those saucer-shaped carriages so admirably suited to the display of vast skirts as they froth over the edge. And here too the 'Lions' and 'Wolves' – the 'heavy swells' – appear, sizing up the ladies of the town. The new model for the 'fille de joie' – the 'grande cocotte' – has gained in assurance quite as much as has the fashionable ideal. Unlike Marie Duplessis she no longer aimed at the appearance of the perfect lady, though like Duplessis, this new model patronized, as such women always had, the most fashionable and expensive dressmakers. M. Worth had considerable trouble in keeping the sheep apart from the goats. Doré catches the knowing swagger of the men, and the effect of billowing movement in women's figures quite superbly, and with far more useful detail than is to be found in the flourishing brushwork of Constantin Guys, 'le peintre de la vie moderne'.

The results of nearly a century of industrial expansion were being used splendidly in England too. 'Money made from muck' was circulating, if not exactly freely, at least in very large quantities among some sections of society. And this was also the great international Exhibition Age. Year after year from 1851 onwards the century marvelled at its own inventive productivity. The showing of these wonders provided centres, attracting thousands, at which one not only saw but was also seen. The magnificently matronly *grande-dame* of the sixties was supported by an increasingly solid masculinity – solid not only in financial standing, but also in appearance. The bulky torso created by the low-waisted frock-coat or the square Tweedside jacket, above peg-top trousers as wide as elephant's legs suggested weight and ponderous movement. The dash and passion of the thirties had been gradually modelled into a firm, heavy dependability, unimaginative but reassuring. The romantic age was dead as far as fashionable appearance was concerned. Materialism was all.

1860 and after

Whatever may be thought of the form which recent criticisms on
dress have taken, and of the evident dissatisfaction with the present
state of things that exist in some circles, it is certain that the attiring
of the body, and its suitable and pleasant adornment, may be classed
amongst 'the lesser arts of life', and as such deserve the attention of all
reasonable men and women.

> Anon.   'Fitness and Fashion' *The Magazine of Art* 1882

The solution for the peculiar difficulties of a puritan society does not
lie in a series of pin-up girls whose breasts, tailored for love, are
explicitly *not* meant for the loving nourishment of their children. It lies
rather in developing greater ease with our clothes on; taking them off
only increases anxiety.

> Margaret Mead   *Male and Female* 1950

It's wonderful what us bits of women do with a string of beads,
but they don't go far with a gentleman.

> Ronald Firbank   *Concerning the Eccentricities of Cardinal Pirelli*

In all directions

From 1860, the complexity of influential interests becomes too great to allow their detailed discussion at this time. A short summary of only the more important of modern developments may indicate both the possibilities open for investigation, and the reason for my reluctance to continue that investigation within the scope of the present work.

With the establishment in 1858 of the House of Worth in the Rue de la Paix women's dress had become a true art, the conscious product of an individual mind which had elected to use the clothes of others as a medium for its own expression. Fashionable dress began to be designed as an entity; conceived at the outset as providing the foundation for an ideal image. This was the rationalization of that earlier instinctive assemblage by an individual of a selection of craftwork arranged for her own satisfaction. The personal art of dress began increasingly to be displayed in the choice made between the work of one artist and that of another. But these artists in dress were, themselves, quite consciously influenced by other artists working in very different media. The introduction of the sewing machine provided a domestic tool to remove manufacture from the exclusive hands of skilled professionals, yet home-dressmaking met sympathetically with mass production. The invention of the paper pattern, the increase in cheaper, more fully illustrated magazines devoted almost entirely to the subject of dress, opened the field ever wider. Exclusiveness and popularization worked together to create a new awareness of clothes and the influences affecting them. By 1896 M. Jean Worth reported:

> . . . one curious development of modern life is that so many people order their clothes in Paris who have perhaps never been within sight of France. People write to us from all over America. We often send photographs of some of our newest creations to all parts of the world. Of late years the lay figure has been brought to an extraordinary state of perfection, and, in many cases, we have *mannequins* exactly reproducing our foreign customers' peculiarities

of form etc. Indeed, this system of fitting has many advantages, especially when, as not unfrequently happens, a client requires twenty to thirty dresses to be made for her at one time. The most successful and newest lay figure is made on the same principle as an india-rubber cushion, and with the help of a pattern bodice, or even the measurements, can be made to express exactly the size and shape required.[1]

At the other end of the scale, it was possible to order by post:

Direct from the Largest Firm of Costume Manufacturers in the World, the John Noble Half-Guinea Costume. Over 1,000 well-paid Workers employed in John Noble's own Factories under the strictest conditions of Sanitation and Cleanliness. These Costumes are made in The John Noble Cheviot Serge (the same quality worn by Miss Böcker at the time of her rescue from the disastrous wreck of the 'Elbe', and sold at 7/6 the dress length) trimmed bold silk cord, as illustration, and are supplied complete for the ridiculous price of 10/6 each, packed in box and sent carriage paid for 9d extra. The most remarkable value ever produced they have secured beyond a doubt The Admiration of the World. The present design excels all previous ones in every respect. The style is better, the cut is superior and the make and finish beyond all criticism.[2]

The middle years of the century had seen the decadence of the Romantic ideal. By 1860 it had become a convention, not a conviction. The sublimation of sexuality was abandoned during the seventies for a dashingly overt erotic appeal in dress. Exaggeration of physical feminine characteristics, rather than their concealment, emphasized still further the different appearance of women from men. No longer an untouchable drifting mass of fragile fabrics, Woman was a fetchingly animated caricature of voluptuousness. The impulse seemed now undoubtedly based upon the seduction, and subjugation, of the male. Women appeared to be achieving the best of all worlds:

For the fashionable beauty life is an endless carnival, and dress a round of disguises. . . . She is a sportswoman, an athlete, a balloon divinity. She is alternately a horsewoman, a huntress, a bold and skilful swimmer; she drives a pair of horses like a charioteer, mounts the roof of a four-in-hand, plays tennis, is at home on a racecourse or the deck of a fast yacht. . . . She is a power at the theatre and the opera; and none is more brilliant at a supper party. Of the modern young lady à la mode . . . none but herself can be the prototype![3]

In the late 1870s – almost exactly a century later than men – women embarked upon a movement towards utility, but without totally renouncing their decorative role. The 'costume', a tailored coat and skirt, allowed women to be women again by day, while they continued to dress-up as 'ladies' in the evening and for galas. Right in the midst of that

1   'La Maison Worth' from *The Lady's Realm*, 1896.

2   *Today*, 26 October 1895 ('A Weekly Magazine Journal' edited by Jerome K. Jerome, London).

3   *The Graphic*, late 1870s, quoted by Bott, Alan, *Our Mothers* (London, 1932).

earlier age which had cherished the ideal of fragile, utterly helpless womanhood, there had already been stirrings of another quite different one. Clara Schumann, the brilliant pianist, had played the works of her husband on a continental tour, and a dazzling group of feminine dancers, Taglioni, Grissi, Elssler, Cerito, Grahn, had stolen all the thunder from the men. Everywhere women novelists were at work to vie with their masculine rivals for popularity; many were disguised by masculine names; and some, if Daumier may be believed, assumed very masculine prerogatives. One of their number, 'George Sand' ('though she may have been to all intents and purposes a man, was not a gentleman')[4] had appeared in public wearing trousers; another, 'George Eliot', lived in open companionship with a man who was not her husband. In 1851, an amazing American lady, Mrs Emilia Jenks Bloomer, had astonished London with her reformed garment, and the pages of *Punch* were filled with gibes at this challenge to current convictions. In the 1870s the independent Sarah Bernhardt wore a satin trouser-suit when sculpting. The door of *The Doll's House* was resoundingly slammed in 1879; women were able to attend their own colleges; and the Suffragette Movement was already under way. From America, the forceful pioneer spirit found expression again in the 'admired ability' of women like Miss Henrietta Stackpole, 'thoroughly launched in journalism . . . who, without parents and without property, had adopted three of the children of an infirm and widowed sister and was paying their school-bills out of the proceeds of her literary labour. . . . Her peculiarly open, surprised-looking eye . . . rested without impudence or defiance, but as if in conscientious exercise of a natural right, upon every object it happened to encounter.'[5]

As women gradually transformed themselves from sublime, pure, angelic beings, into distinctly dangerous predatory animals, whose flounced and furbelowed tails lashed viciously with every brisk advancing step, the earlier Romantic veneration of woman changed to fear. After the intense and mystic eroticism, exemplified by Wagner's union of opposites in the final sacrifice of death, came a violent, infatuated hatred. Whatever men thought of women in particular, for the artist, Woman in general showed:

> a beauty wrought out from within upon the flesh, the deposit,
> little cell by cell, of strange thoughts and fantastic reveries and
> exquisite passions. . . . This beauty into which the soul with all its
> maladies has passed . . .

For Walter Pater, this beauty was found in Leonardo's *Mona Lisa*, 'the embodiment of the old fancy, the symbol of the modern idea.'[6] To Edvard Munch, the painter of *The Vampire*, she was:

> . . . the woman who demands everything for her own sake.
> Insatiable in her lust for what she feels gives life meaning.[7]

Octave Uzanne found her portrayed by George de Feure as: '. . . the woman of a thousand curves, a thousand fascinations, consumed by a selfish love, given to all excesses, the trunk whence all the vices spring,

4 James, Henry, comment on George Sand quoted in Beerbohm, M., *Around Theatres*, 'Kipling's Entire' (London, 1953).

5 James, Henry, *The Portrait of a Lady* (New York, 1880).

6 Pater, Walter, *The Renaissance* (London, 1876).

7 *See* Stang, N., *Edvard Munch* (Oslo, 1972).

the source of all the ills, the soul of every forbidden delight'.[8]

In the art of the Symbolists and their sympathizers the culminating effects of the Romantic movement celebrated woman as the *Femme Fatale*. Salome, the personification of perverted destructive feminine desire, and the grotesque possessive prostitute, became the cult figures for the age. The wilful Spirit of Nature had become a monster. This dangerously seductive being had her fashionable appearances in the Art Nouveau splendours which brought the nineteenth century to a close and opened the twentieth – a final defiant flourish of the romantically motivated establishment in the face of modernity.

During the 1880s, the ideological challenge to the materialism of established fashion had been joined by an aesthetic challenge in the Dress-Reform Movement. Having originated privately as an unformulated, romantic revolt among the intensely 'Medieval' women of the 'Morris set', it was later publicly led by the artists G. F. Watts and E. W. Godwin, and popularized by the lectures of Oscar Wilde, whose notoriety had been assured by the fortuitous publicity of Gilbert and Sullivan's *Patience*.

Aestheticism affected the ideal of masculinity as well as that of femininity:

A Guardsman at home is always, if anything, rather more luxuriously accommodated than a young Duchess.[9]

Too languid, as he lay there on his divan, to raise the vinaigrette to his nostrils, he was one who had served his country through more than one campaign on the boiling plains of the Sahara; he who, in the palace of a *nouveau riche*, had refused the bedchamber assigned to him, on the plea that he could not sleep under a false Fragonard, had often camped *à la belle étoile* in the waste places of Central Asia;[10]

This strangely uncertain generation, the product of the complete dichotomy imposed by Romanticism (and beginning to be unhappily aware of the antagonism implicit in that unnatural division) provided the case histories upon which the work of Krafft-Ebbing, and later Sigmund Freud were based.

With the new century came another aesthetic challenge from the violent brilliance of *Les Fauves*. Popularized by the designers for Diaghilev's *Ballet Russe*, who combined it with a lavish oriental exoticism, it received also a fashionable statement in the work of the couturier Paul Poiret, who took the stiffening out of stays even for the unemancipated woman.

The complete havoc of World War I began nothing new: it merely speeded a general process of social and aesthetic disintegration started fifty years before. The personal creations of the sculptor Brancusi and the painter Modigliani were adapted to the needs of a sophisticated public by decorative draughtsmen of the calibre of Georges Barbier and Benito, affecting the way women wanted to look, and this in its turn led to a wider acceptance of the more unusual original expressions.

The influence of other abstract art appeared in the cutting of clothing on abstract lines, bearing little recognizable relationship to the human body. Only a skilled couturier could invent, or predict, the final appearance of

8 Uzanne, Octave, 'On the drawings of M. Georges de Feure', in *Studio*, Vol. XII (London, 1898).

9 'Ouida', *Under Two Flags* (London, 1867).

10 Beerbohm, Max, 'Ouida', from *More* (London, 1899).

the extraordinary shapes which were laid out on the cutting-table. Interest in the subtle form of dress at last supplanted completely the age-old interest in decoration. The placing of seams was avidly studied and changed from season to season. The influences of Cubism, Futurism, Orphism and Surrealism all contributed their effectiveness to dress, not merely in the matter of fabric design.

During the 1920s, bodies were finally released from clothing which controlled them. Suits and dresses skimmed over their surfaces in a 'fit' which an earlier age would have considered far too large. The whole principle of clothing had radically changed for the first time in 600 years. The past was not, however, totally rejected. Complex shaping had become an integral and essential part of every garment, but that shaping now ceased to affect the body, which regained its individual importance. The final appearance of the dress was once again dependent upon the body's shape. Sport, exercise and sunbathing replaced padding, whalebone and compression as the principal aids to an ideal figure. During the twenties also came definite efforts to heal the breach between the sexes. The over-emphasis of differences had resulted in almost open war during the late nineteenth century. Most extreme reactions had been coupled with neurosis. Militant demands for women's rights, and a self-consciously cultivated male homosexuality were both reflected in the dress of influential minority groups. Now the new attempts at a more balanced view of human nature among the *avant-garde* were generally noted satirically. In 1925 *Le Rire* illustrated the cryptic comment of an elderly *roué*: 'Oh, pardon me, miss, I thought you were a pansy'. And in 1930, 'Miss Runcible wore trousers and Miles touched up his eyelashes in the dining-room of the hotel where they stopped for luncheon. So they were asked to leave'.[11] But the way back towards some equilibrium was being sought.

In the thirties, the full exploitation of the bias-cutting of fabric allowed every natural undulation of the naked, unsupported female body to show clearly beneath it. 'Streamlined' was the adulatory adjective applied to feminine figures as well as to cars, and the design of furniture. Meanwhile, experiments were made with masculine resort and leisure-wear to reintroduce more obvious colouring, and a freedom of invention not permitted for more than a century. The influence of the cinema had reached immense proportion, not only in its widespread picturing of a dream existence, but in the effect it had on general grooming. The ideal images, smooth, pressed and polished with never a hair out of place, produced a society more self-consciously aware of 'finish' than any before.

The exigencies of World War II forced exclusive couturiers to design for mass industrial production, and any woman who could acquire sufficient coupons was able to buy, for a very modest sum, a well-made garment, conceived by a first-rate artist of international repute.

The financial freedom which came to youth in the 1950s began a competitive system of age-grouping, to replace the disappearing snobbery of class-consciousness. For the re-emerging male (notably eye-catching after a century of retirement) clothes often took on the importance of primitive tribal identification, in a world aspiring to complete sophistication. The rejection of all earlier romantic division of the roles of male and female, augmented by the popularity of the revelations of psycho-

11 Waugh, Evelyn, *Vile Bodies* (London, 1930).

analysis, helped to confuse people, who expressed their confusion in dress. This dress further muddled an older generation which declared itself unable to distinguish the boys from the girls. Exaggerated differences had demanded at last the reaction of exaggerated reconciliation. About a century earlier, Florence Nightingale had perceptively observed:

> In the conventional society (which men have made for women, and women have accepted) . . . the system dooms minds to incurable infancy, others to silent misery. . . . In society men and women meet to be idle. Is it extraordinary that they do not know each other, and that in their mutual ignorance they form no surer friendships?[12]

Now the reconciliation was made in dress, and in behaviour, described as 'Unisex'. Attempts were made to prove that there were no appreciable differences at all between the temperament and outlook of the two sexes, and even that their physical and biological characteristics were not as completely opposite as had been recently supposed. While a young wife could earn a living as a test-pilot, her husband happily stayed at home to bath the baby. At the mercy of commercial exploitation, they themselves were not too much confused about their physical sex – merely about how active it should be, and about what 'male' and 'female' really meant.

Distinct divisions between architecture, sculpture and painting also began to fade. A house was not an agglomeration of cubic rooms, but a free moulding of space by the balancing of mass and void. Sculpture was built by bolting girders into a structure. A 'painting' ceased to be an arrangement of colours on canvas, but could be realized as a three-dimensional environment of coloured light, within which the viewer moved. Or, flat, it could make him dizzy and feel as if he was moving while he was standing still. 'Op', 'Pop' and 'Mixed Media' were titles as applicable to clothing as to other art. God was declared to be dead. Public destruction was discussed as a valid expression; while the artist himself was put forward as a work of art.

Curiously, neither experiments with chemically produced fibres or solid 'plastics', nor the technology which put men on the Moon, have so far had any but peripheral effects upon the way we dress. Our concern is clearly concentrated upon the exploration of problems presented by proximity, increased population, and the high speed of communication which is so rapidly shrinking this world. The opening-up of the universe has hardly distracted attention from more immediate concerns at home. All these aspects of a world of doubt, unease, trouble and alarm have found their counterpart in what we wear, and the full exploration of the cross-currents flowing back and fourth between dress, art and society during the last hundred years would require a volume much larger than the present. Writing recently, Peter Brook has said of the dramatic author:

> The more clearly he recognises the missing links in his relationships – the more accurately he experiences that he is never deep enough in enough aspects of the theatre; that his necessary seclusion is also his prison – the more then can he begin to find ways of connecting

12   *See* Housman, L., *The Great Victorians*, Vol. 2, edited by H. J. and Hugh Massingham (London, 1932).

strands of observation and experience which at present remain unlinked.[13]

The same attitude of mind befits the student of costume: the same links can be found in aspects of dress. Shakespeare's hackneyed phrase that 'All the world's a stage, and all the men and women merely players', has constant application for this study, for dress makes actors of us all. Like good 'Method' players, we expect our costumes to be clothes, and to function in two ways: to work upon our own minds, helping us to adjust to the role we have elected to play, so that its effect will be intensified upon the audience, which will in turn adjust its reactions to what we wear. Like actors we work by instinct and technique, both of which will assure that whatever the demands of our particular character, the individual costume will remain only a unit in the complete production, which is illuminated by the spirit of the age in which we live. Also, like actors, while concentrating on our parts, we frequently forget the more important reasons which controlled the selection of our clothes. These wider issues seem irrelevant at the time and we are aware only of more immediate, intimate matters. Samuel Pepys, for example, recorded in 1663:

> To church, where I found that my coming in a periwig did not prove so strange as I was afraid it would, for I thought that all the church would presently have cast their eyes all upon me.[14]

Such a mixture of apprehension at attracting too much notice, and bitter disappointment at having attracted none, is a timeless factor involved in the wearing of clothes, and has a place in the personal experience of all. In 1822 the romantic painter Delacroix, who, like Pepys was a very dressy man, confided to his journal:

> It is most extraordinary, I've done nothing all day but worry over the new coat which I tried on this morning; the one that fitted so badly. I find myself staring at every coat I pass in the street.

That almost maniac compulsion, that obsessive eagerness with which any one, in any age, who is only faintly concerned about dress, must examine other people's clothes to see if their own too are similar, strikes a sympathetic chord. These are the things which dominate the mind immediately when acquiring new clothes – not the many influences which make the appearance of each one of us a statement of period as well as of personal style. Examine and explain these statements as we will, it must be admitted, that as in any art, there remains some quite inexplicable mystery to account for their attraction. It cannot be fully grasped, though it may be accepted and enjoyed.

In 1935, Rose Macaulay included dress among a selection of *Personal Pleasures*. In a piece of writing which admirably places clothes in a correct perspective, I leave the final words to her:

> How handsome it looks, my dress, fresh from its maker's hands!
> How elegant, how eximious, how smug, how quaintly fashioned,

13 Brook, Peter, *The Empty Space* (London, 1968).

14 Pepys, Samuel, op. cit., 8 November 1663.

see also, 1 July 1660:

'This morning came home my fine Camlett cloak, with gold buttons, and a silk suit which cost me much money and I pray God to make me able to pay for it.'

how all that there is of the modish! How like other people I shall appear when I wear it! With what respect they will regard me, saying one to another, Look, do you see that woman? She knows how to dress; she is in the mode; indeed, she looks very well. I think I have at other times seen her in dresses three, four, even five year old, altered, as she believes, but not really, to the discerning eye, altered to matter, for they still remain of their epoch, and insufferable to people of good taste and modern outlook, now that there is such gaudy going and such new fashions every day. But to-day she really has a *new* dress, and a *good* dress; to-day she really is a Well-Dressed Woman. . . . Strange, what a singular effect the body's outer wrapping has on the mind, how it elevates or depresses the termless spirit of man, exalting it to preen its feathers among the plumy angels, abasing it to creep the earth with meanest worm.

Foolish questions have been asked about this matter by philosophers and moralists since human beings began to ask foolish questions at all . . . Why . . . the philosophers and moralists desire to know, should we that are earth, ashes and dust prick up ourselves so peacockly? They are seldom answered, since the earth, ashes and dust is too busy pricking up itself to pause to reply to foolish questions.

Bibliography

For the convenience of the student this bibliography is arranged according to subject-matter, being divided into two main sections, the use of which is meant to be comparative and complementary.

Dress and Fashion

Boucher, François *A History of Costume in the West* Thames & Hudson, London 1967

Davenport, Millia *The Book of Costume* Crown Publishers, New York 1964

Kybalová, L., Herbenova, O. and Lamarova, M. *The Pictorial Encyclopaedia of Fashion*, Crown Publishers, New York 1969; Hamlyn, London 1969

Payne, Blanche *History of Costume* Harper & Row, New York 1965

Bell, Quentin *On Human Finery* Hogarth Press, London 1947

Cunnington, C. Willet *The Art of English Costume* Collins, London 1948

Flügel, J. C. *The Psychology of Clothes* International Universities Press, New York 1969; Hogarth Press, London 1950

Gernsheim, Alison *Fashion and Reality* Hillary House, New York 1963; Faber & Faber, London 1963

Hiler, Hilaire *From Nudity to Raiment* Simpkin Marshall, London 1929

Laver, James *Taste and Fashion* Harrap, London 1945

Moore, Doris Langley *The Woman in Fashion* Batsford, London 1949

Moore, Doris Langley *Fashion through Fashion Plates* Clarkson Potter, New York 1971; Ward Lock, London 1971

Arnold, Janet *Patterns of Fashion* (2 vols.) Wace, London 1964, 1966

Thornton, Peter *Baroque and Rococo Silks* Faber & Faber, London 1965

Waugh, Norah *Corsets and Crinolines* Theatre Arts Books, New York 1954, Batsford, London 1970

Waugh, Norah *The Cut of Men's Clothes* Theatre Arts Books, New York 1964; Faber & Faber, London 1964

Waugh, Norah *The Cut of Women's Clothes* Theatre Arts Books, New York 1968; Faber & Faber, London 1968

Art and Society

Clark, Kenneth *Civilization* Harper & Row, New York 1970; John Murray, London 1969

Dunwell, Wilfred *Music and the European Mind* London 1962

Duvignaud, Jean *The Sociology of Art* Paladin, London 1972

Hauser, Arnold *The Social History of Art* (4 vols.) Random House, New York 1962; Routledge & Kegan Paul, London 1962

Read, Herbert *The Meaning of Art* Faber & Faber, London 1969

Brion, Marcel *Art of the Romantic Era* Praeger, New York 1966; Thames & Hudson, London 1966

Collingwood, R. G. *The Principles of Art* Oxford University Press, New York 1938; London 1938

Dresden, Samual *Humanism in the Renaissance* McGraw-Hill, New York 1966; Weidenfeld & Nicolson, London 1968

Henderson, George *Gothic* Penguin, Harmondsworth 1967

Honour, Hugh *Neo-classicism* Penguin, Harmondsworth 1968

Kimball, Fiske *The Creation of Rococo* W. W. Norton, New York 1964

Levey, Michael *Early Renaissance* Penguin, Harmondsworth 1970

Panofsky, Erwin *Renaissance and Renascences in Western Art* Harper & Row, New York 1969; Paladin, London 1970

Praz, Mario *On Neo-classicism* Northwestern University Press, Evanston, Illinois 1969; Thames & Hudson, London 1969

Read, Herbert *Art and Society* Schocken Books, New York 1967; Faber & Faber, London 1967

Rosenblum, Robert *Transformations in Late Eighteenth Century Art* Princeton University Press, New Jersey 1967

Sewter, A. C. *Baroque and Rococo Art* Thames & Hudson, London 1972

Shearman, John *Mannerism* Penguin, Harmondsworth 1970

Smart, Alistair *The Renaissance and Mannerism in Italy* Harcourt Brace Jovanovich, New York 1971; Thames & Hudson, London 1972

Smart, Alistair *The Renaissance and Mannerism outside Italy* Thames & Hudson, London 1972

Talmon, J. L. *Romanticism and Revolt* Harcourt Brace Jovanovich, New York 1967; Thames & Hudson, London 1967

Wölfflin, Heinrich *Renaissance and Baroque* Cornell Press, New York 1967; Fontana, London 1964

Index

911